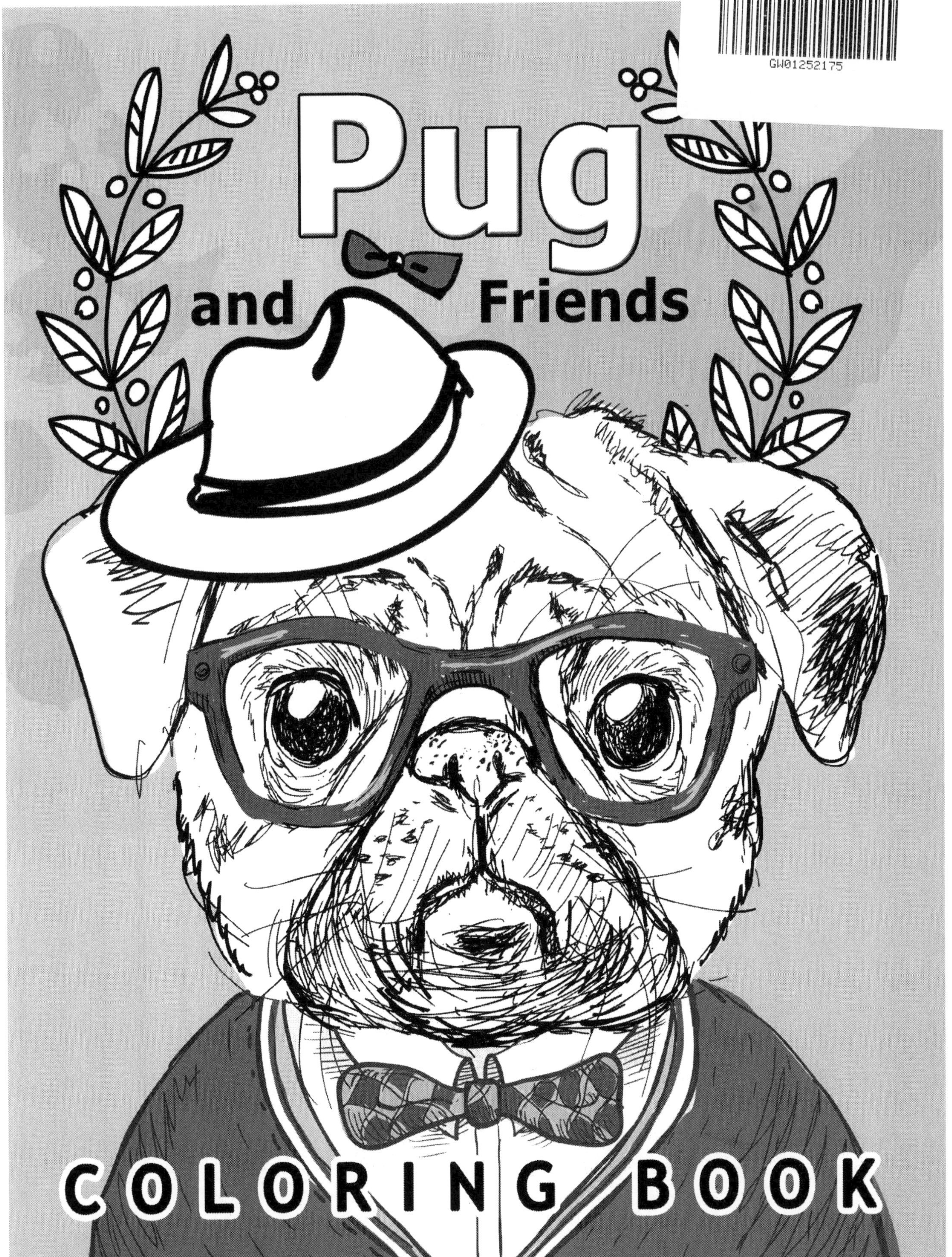
Pug
and Friends
COLORING BOOK

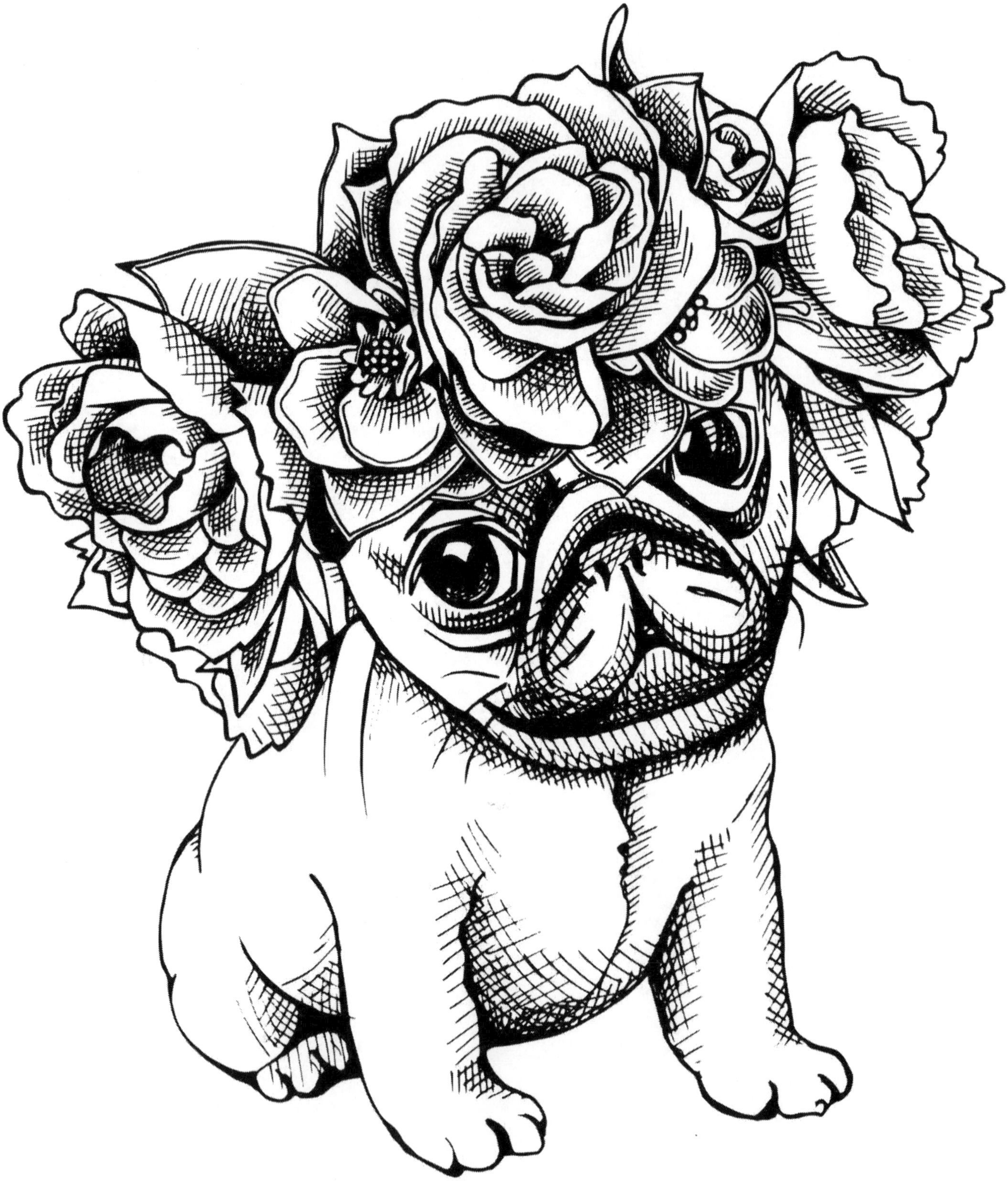

TEST YOUR COLOR

1.

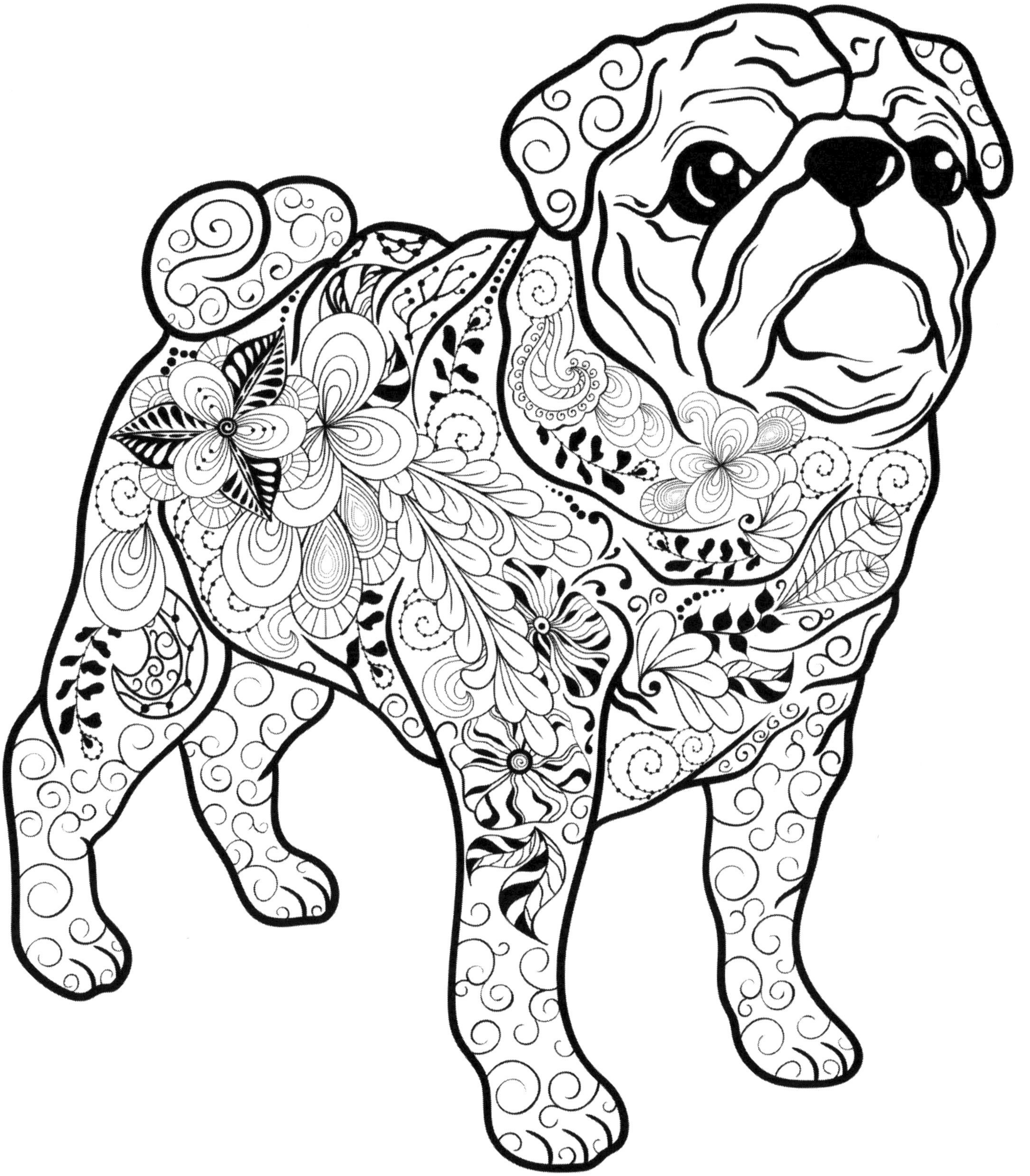

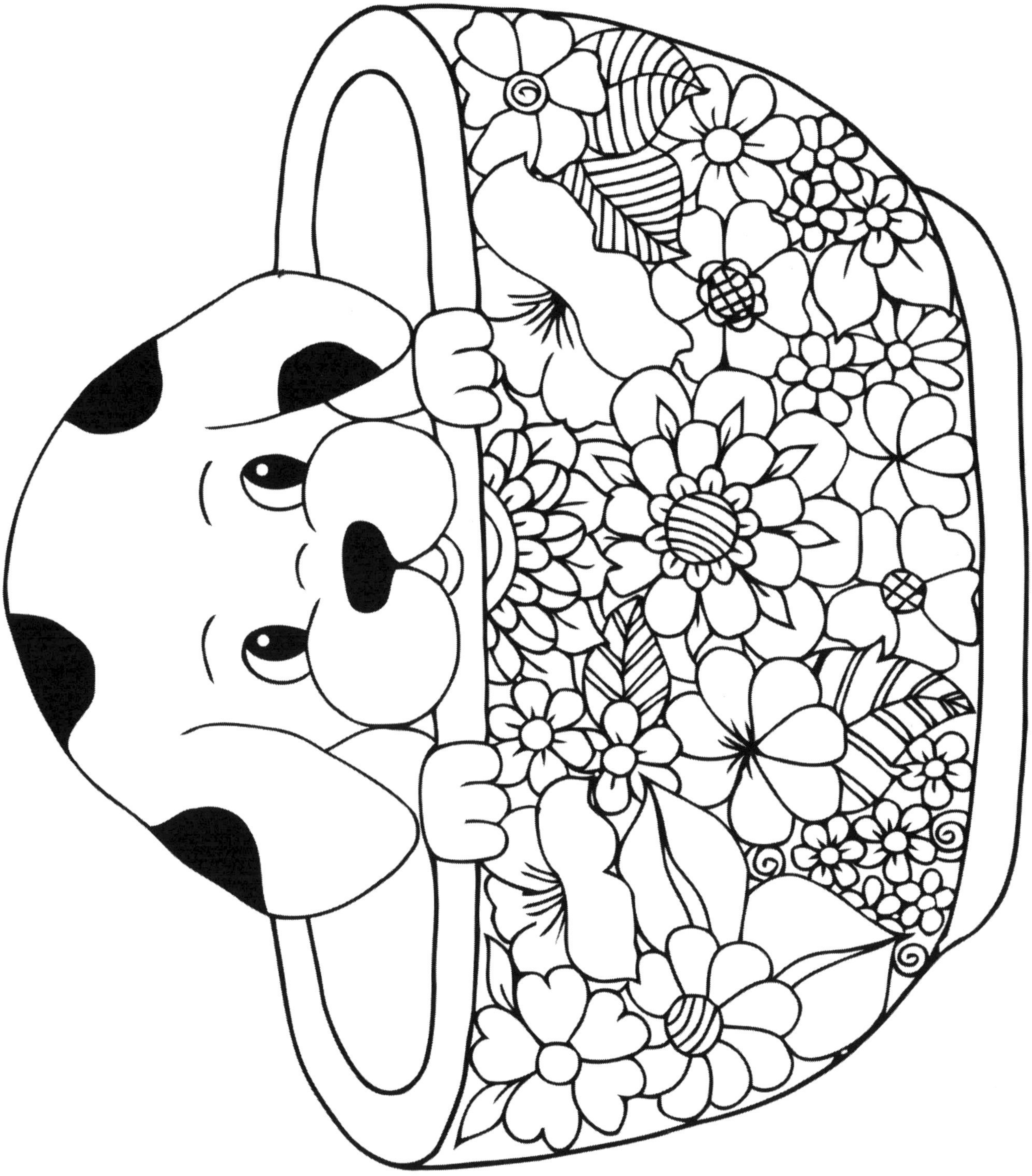

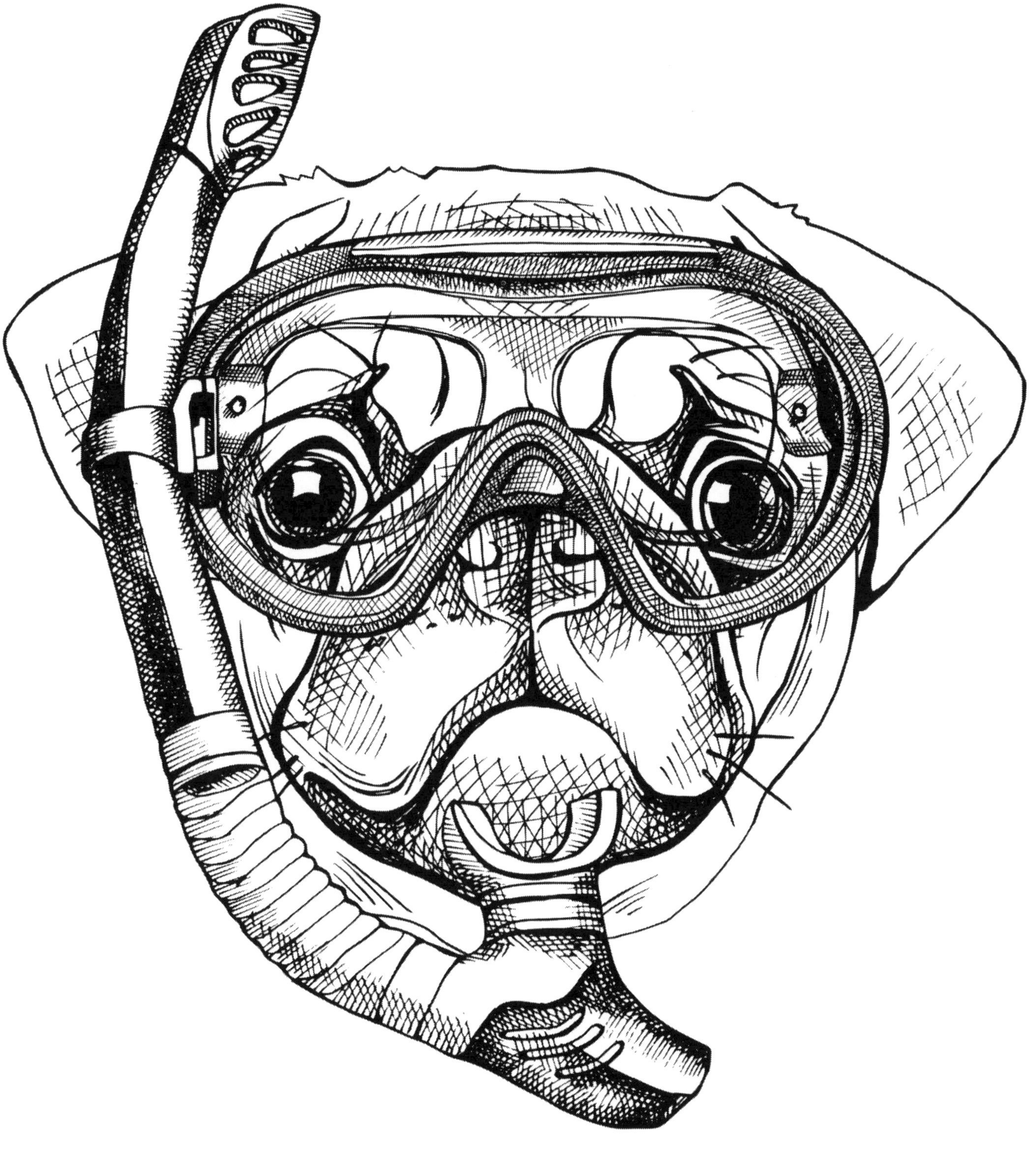

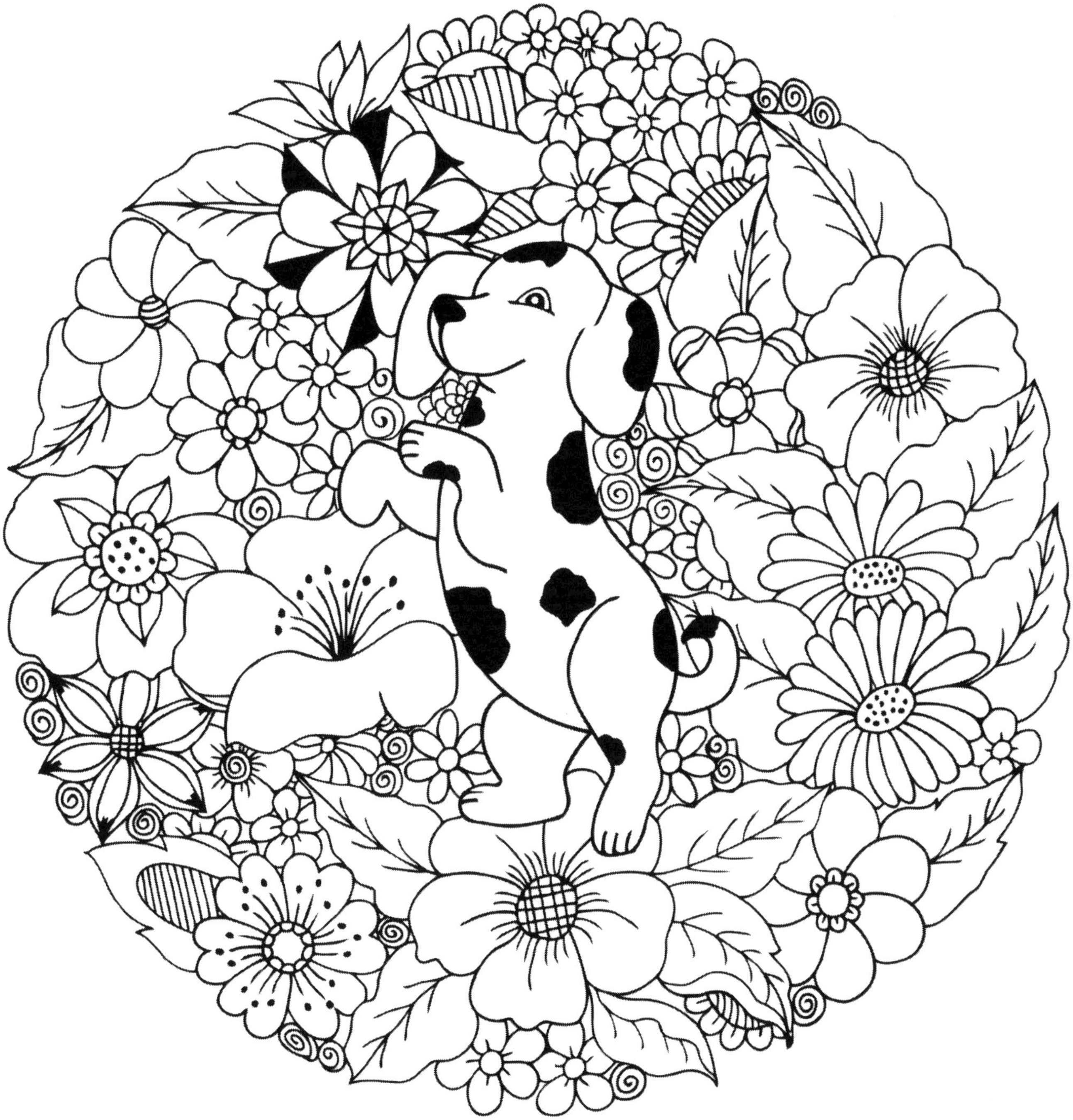

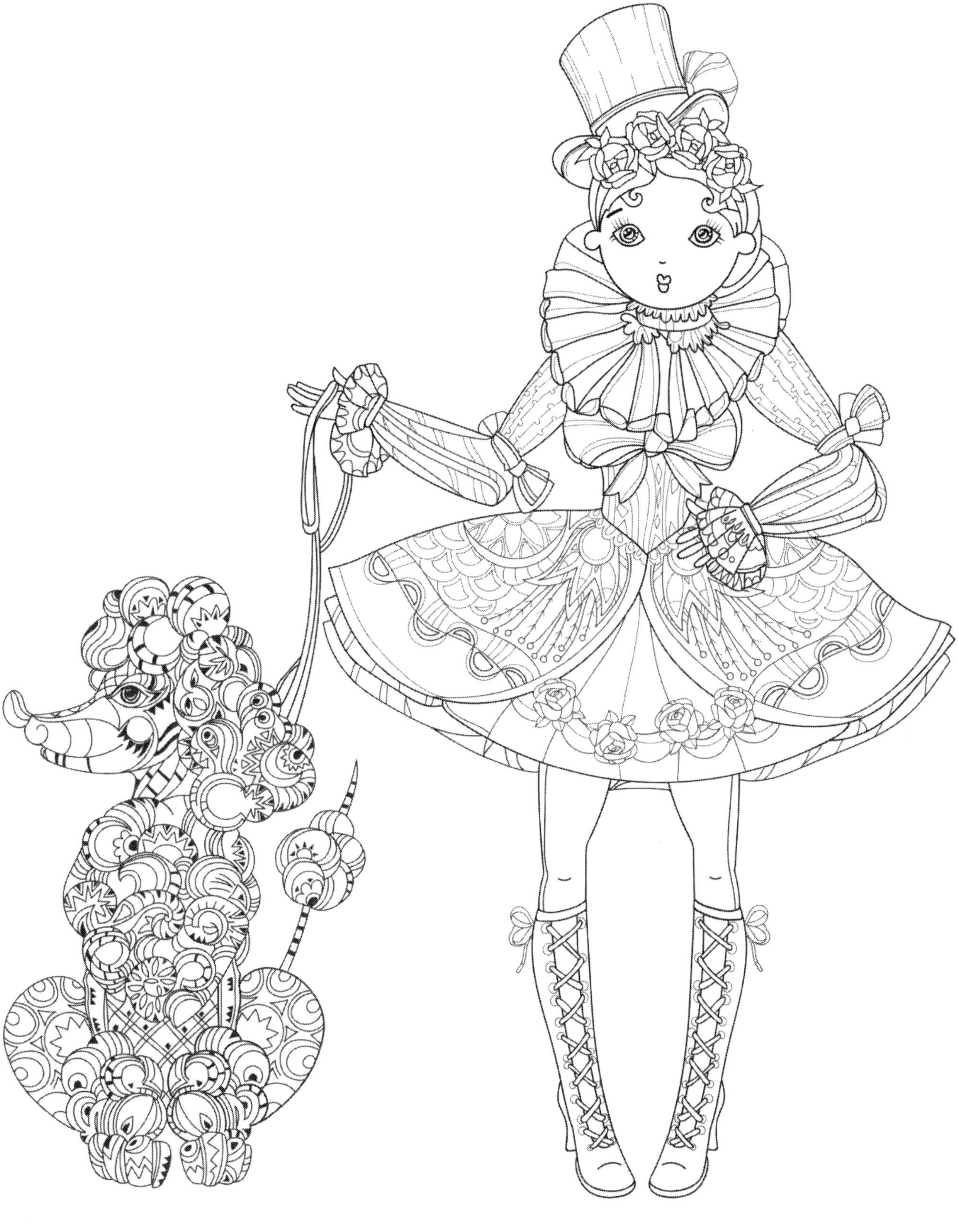

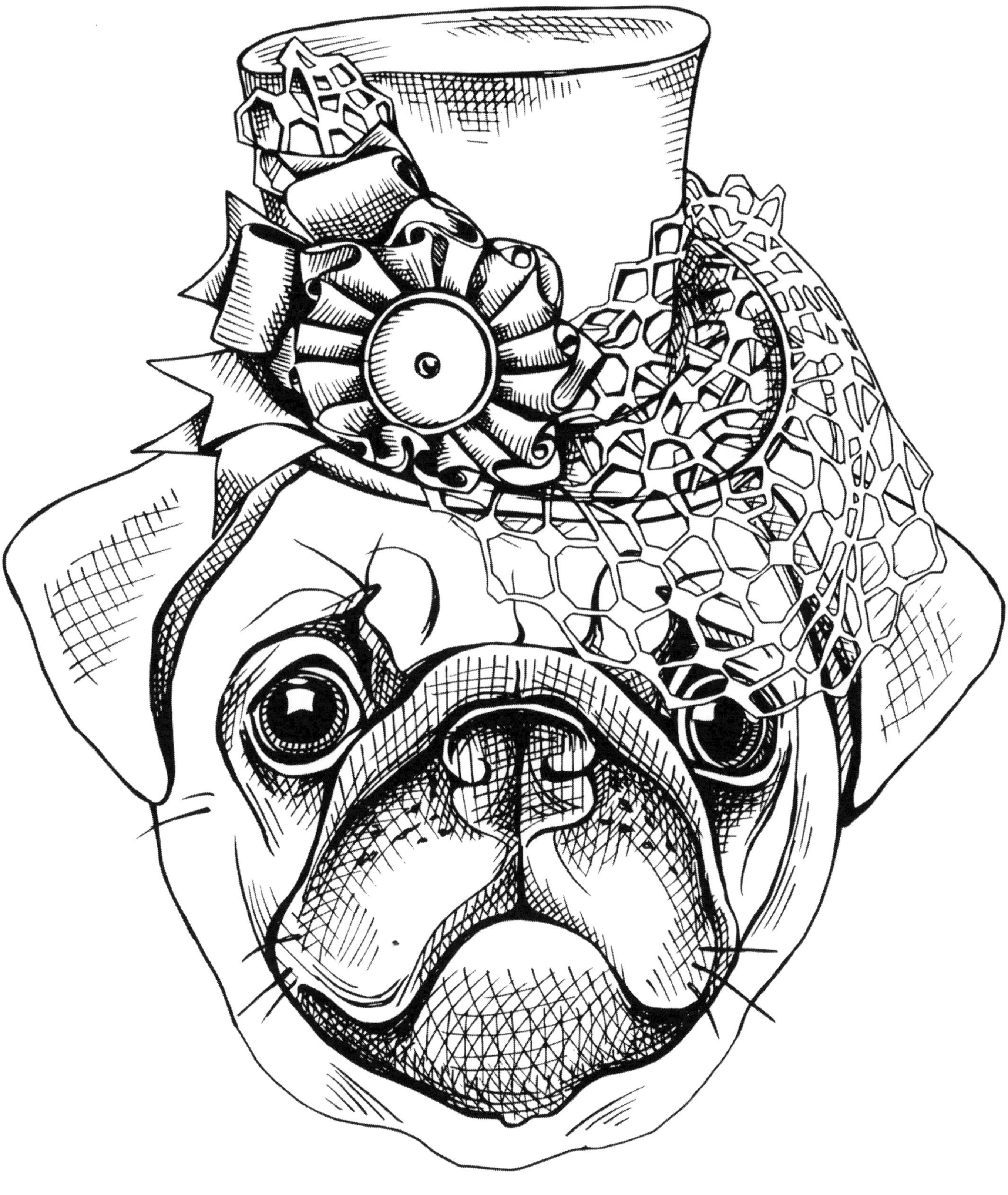

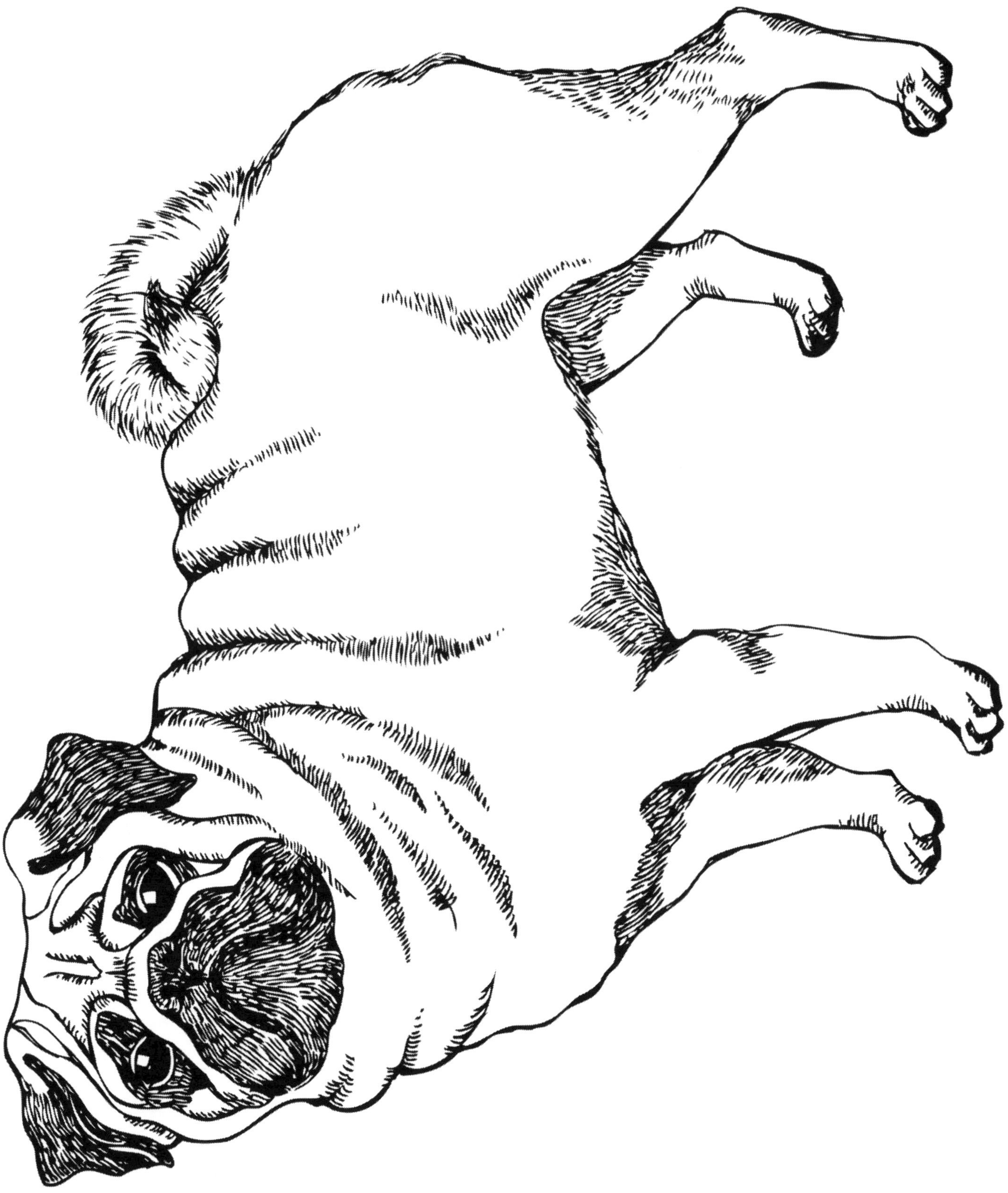

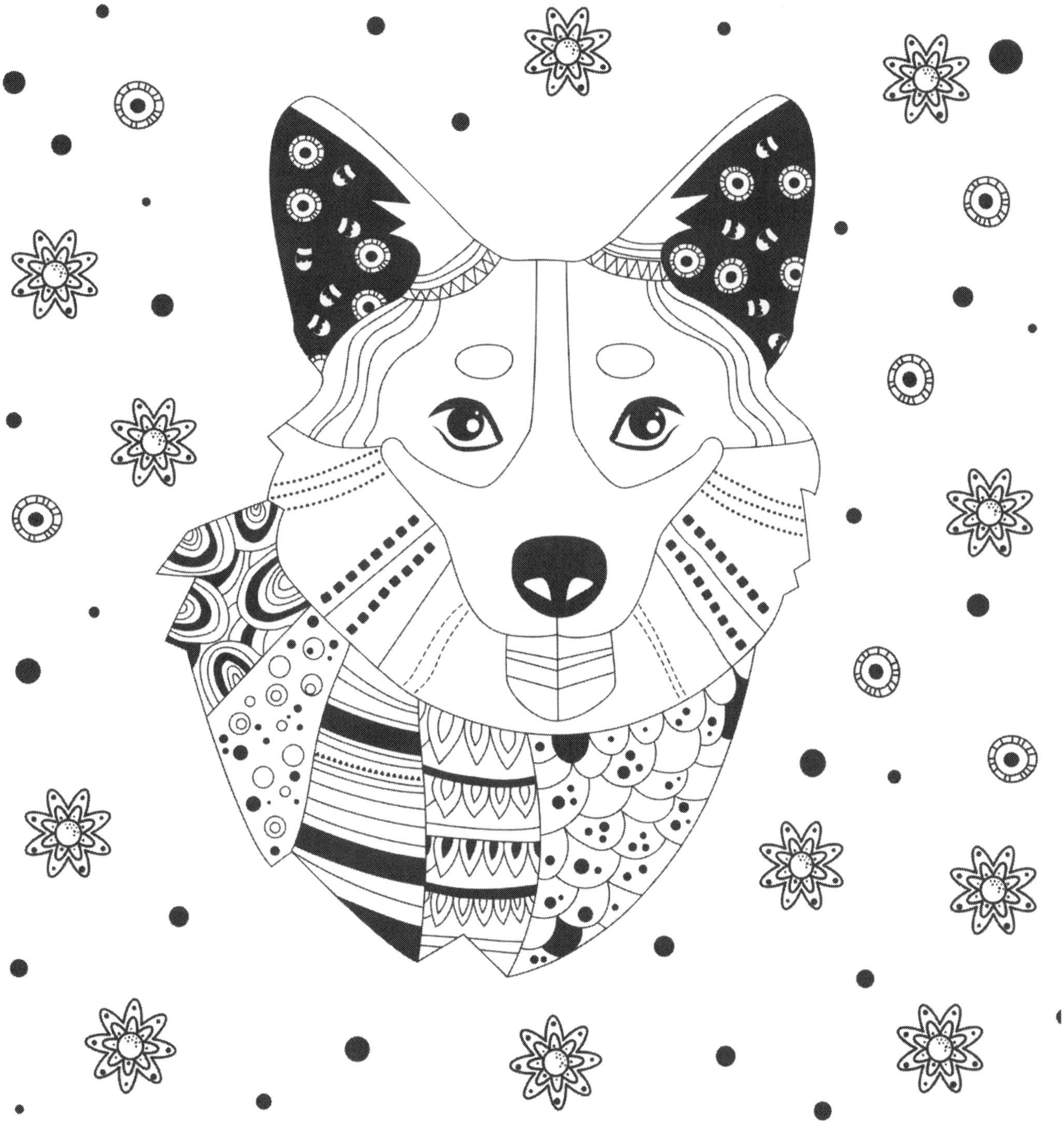

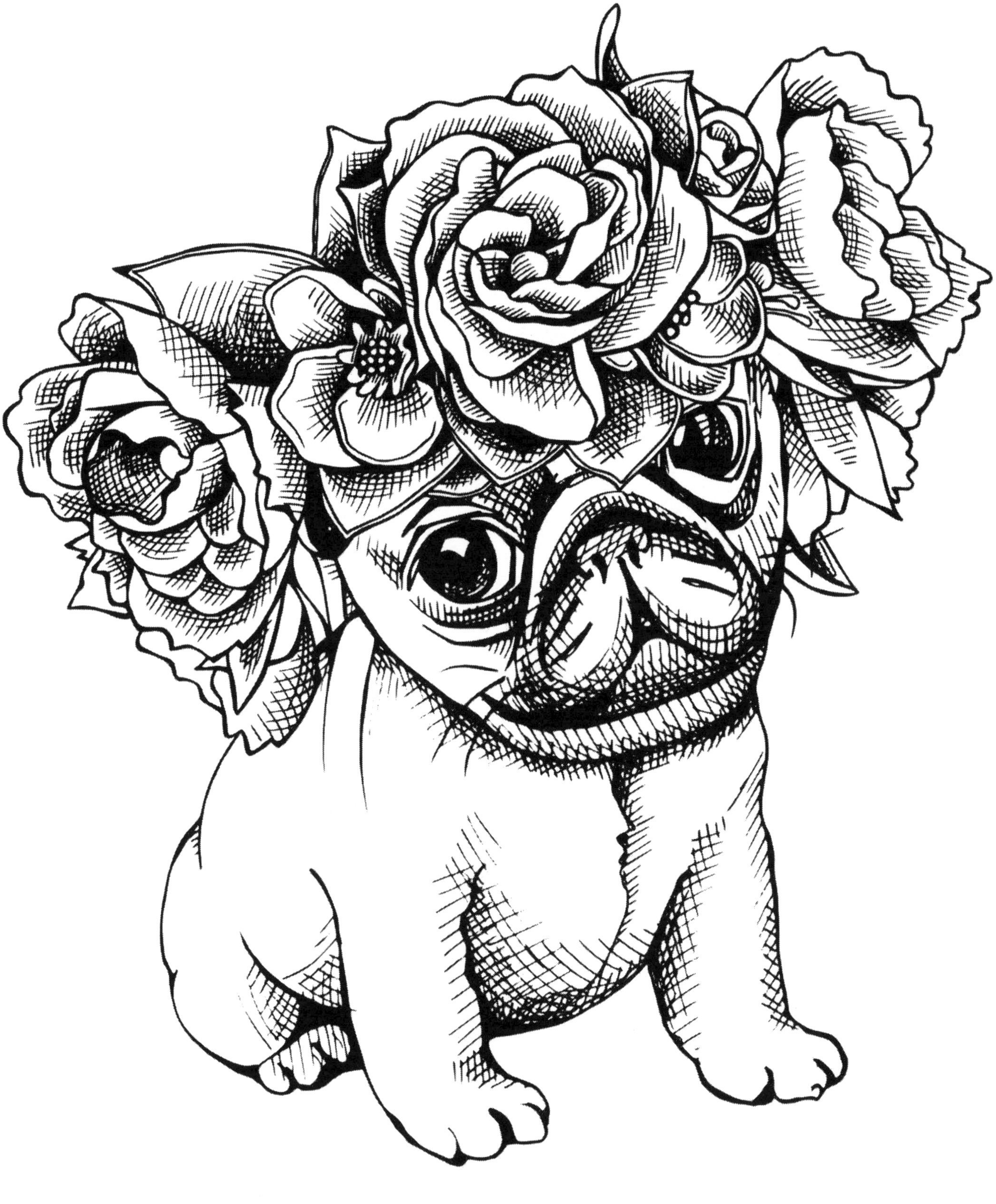

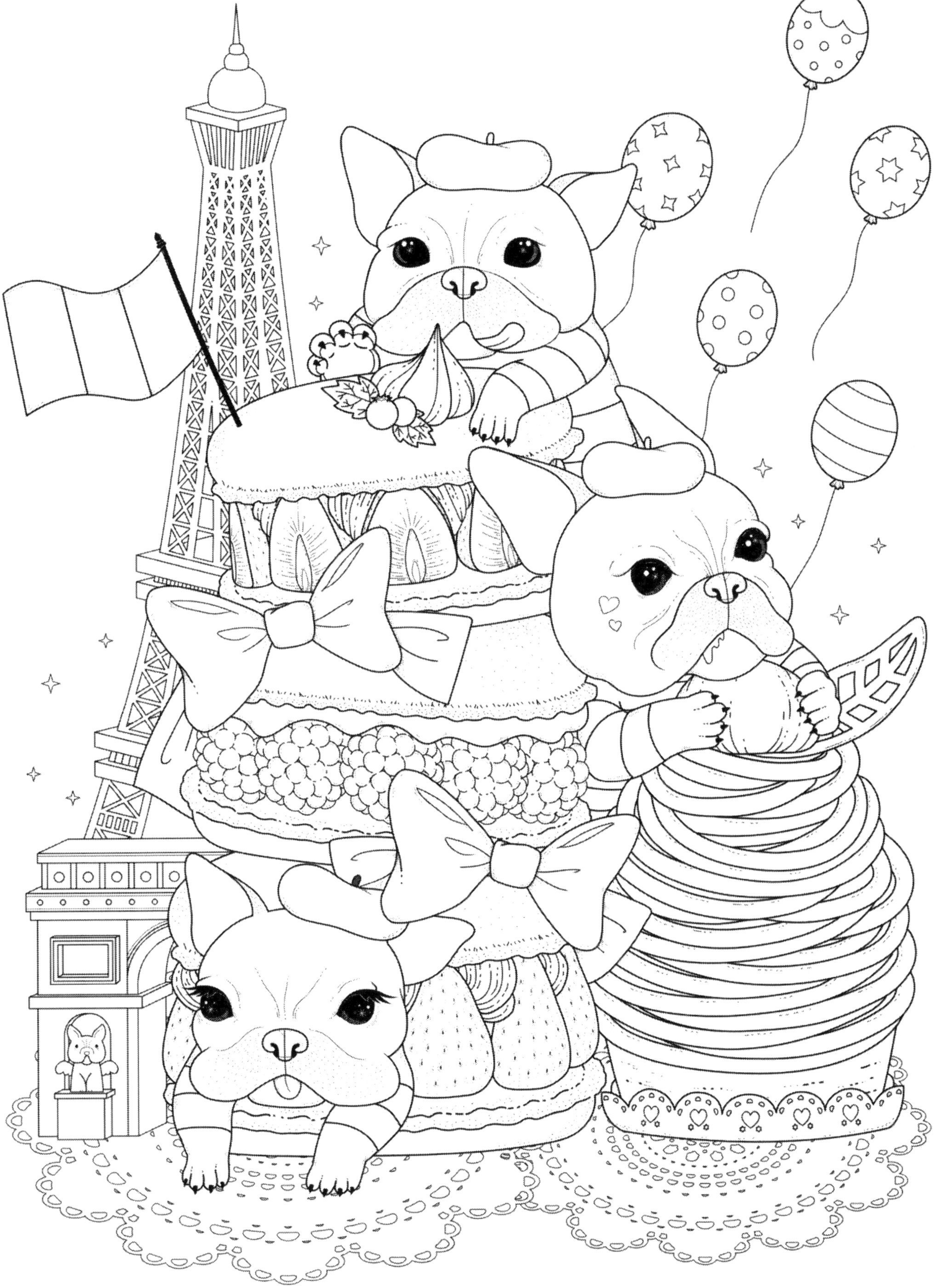

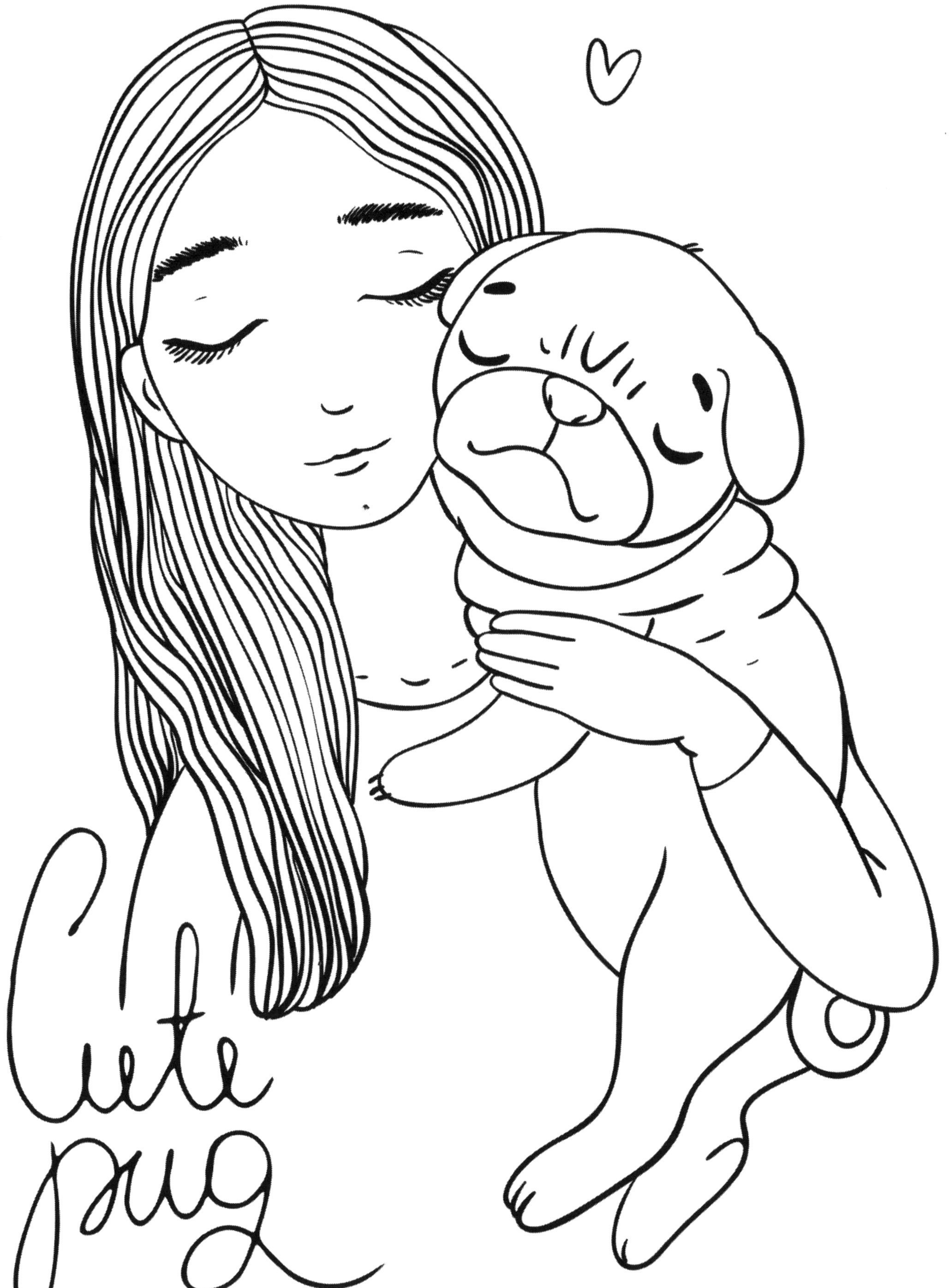
Cute
pug

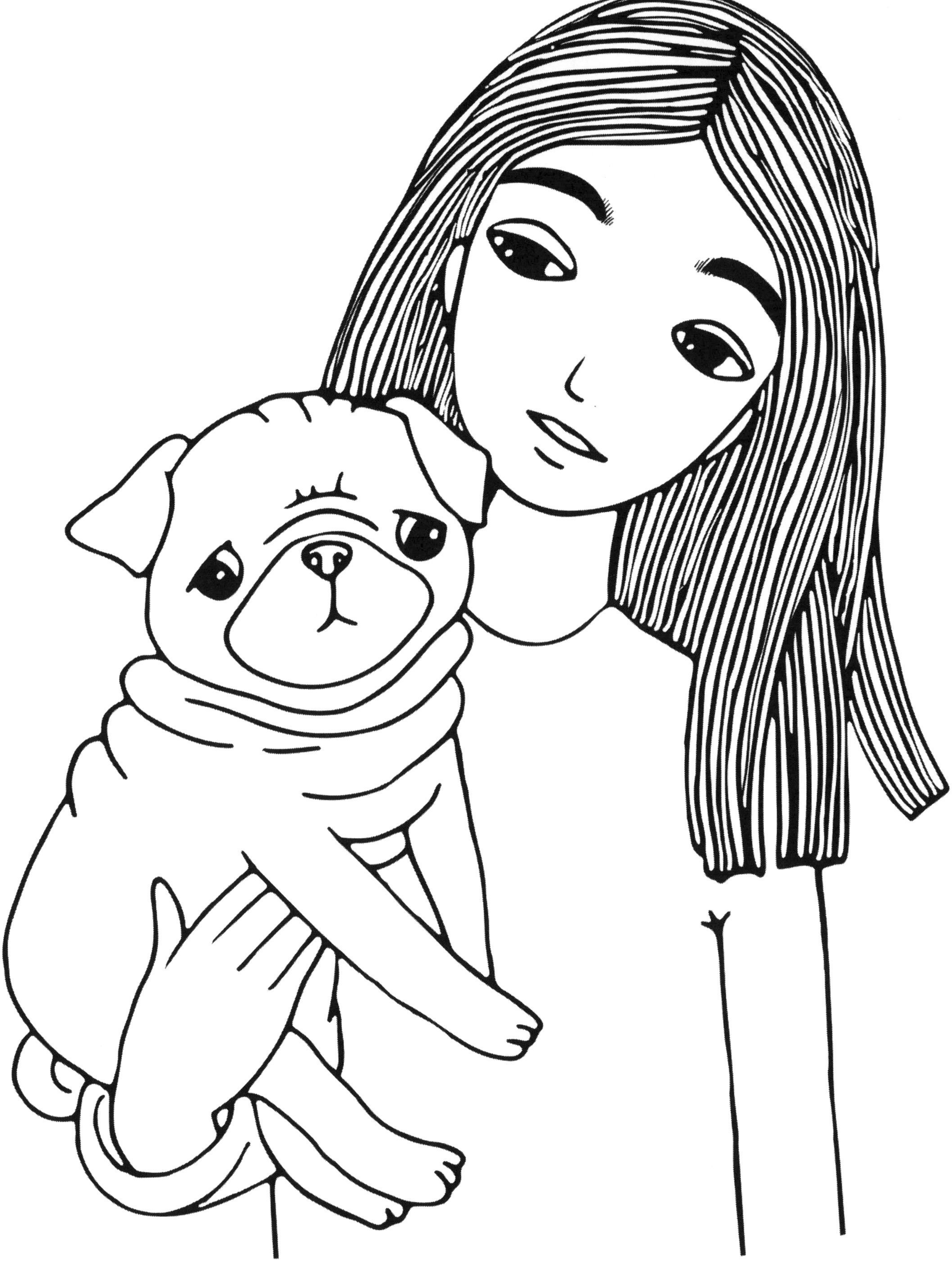

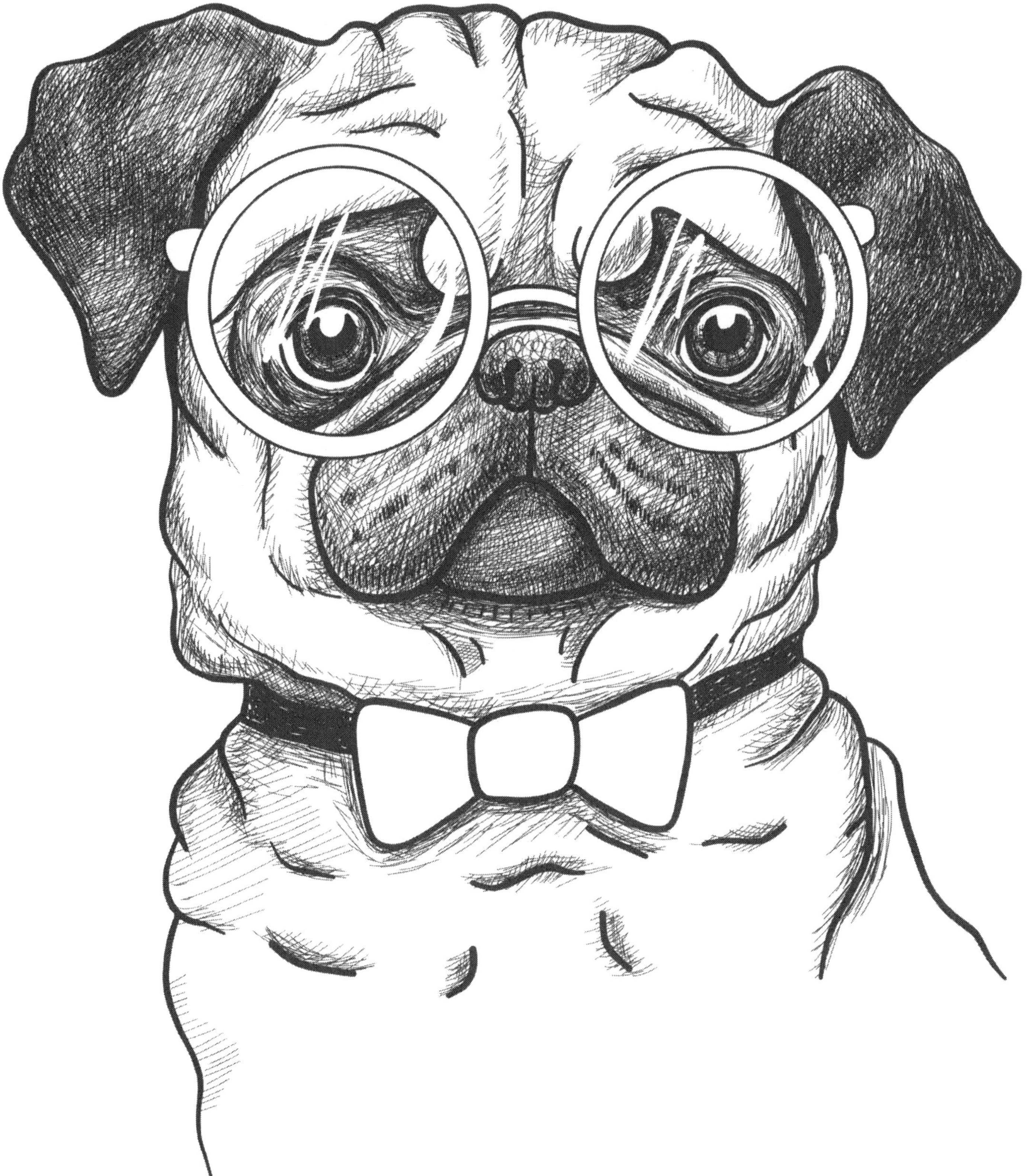

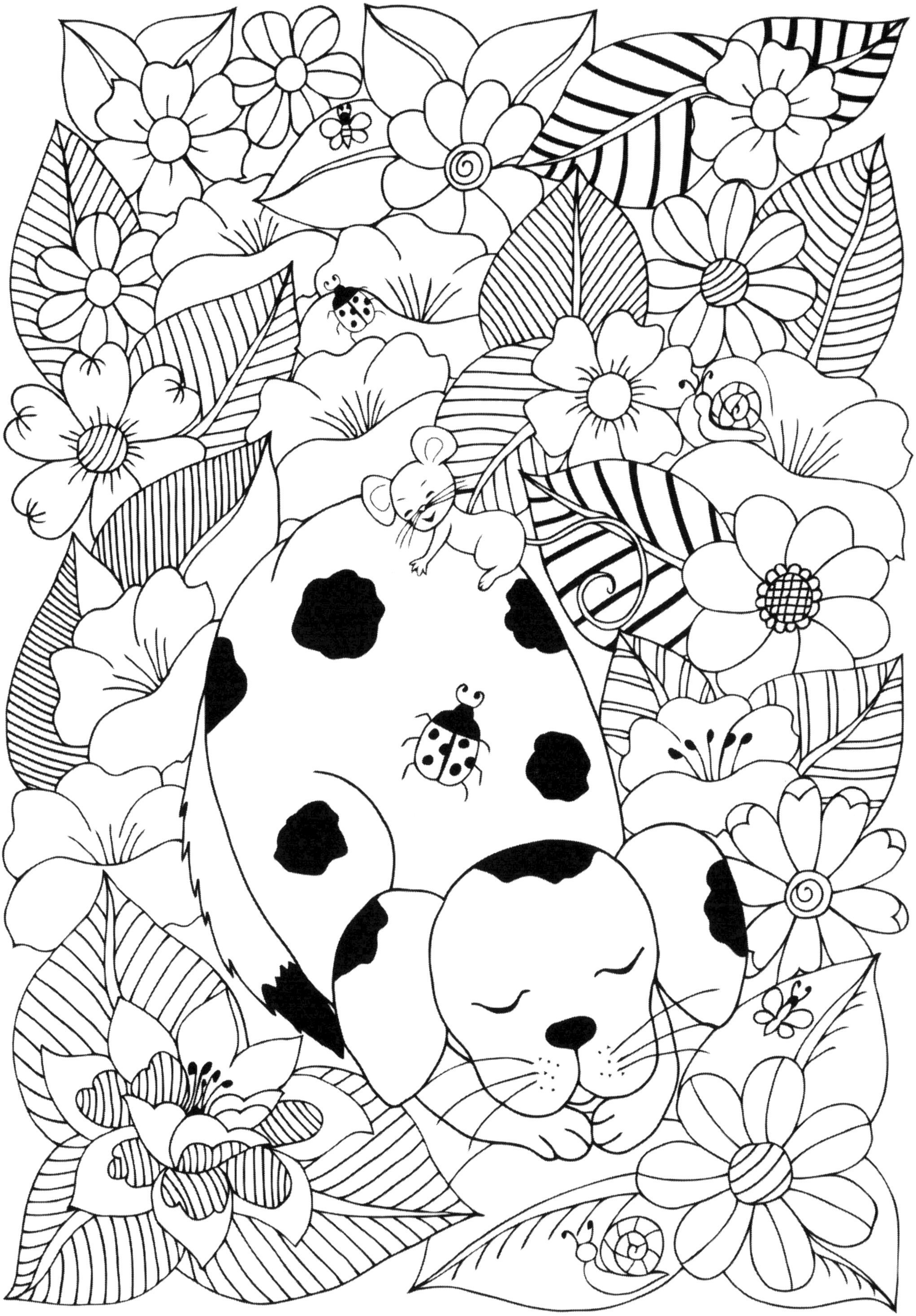

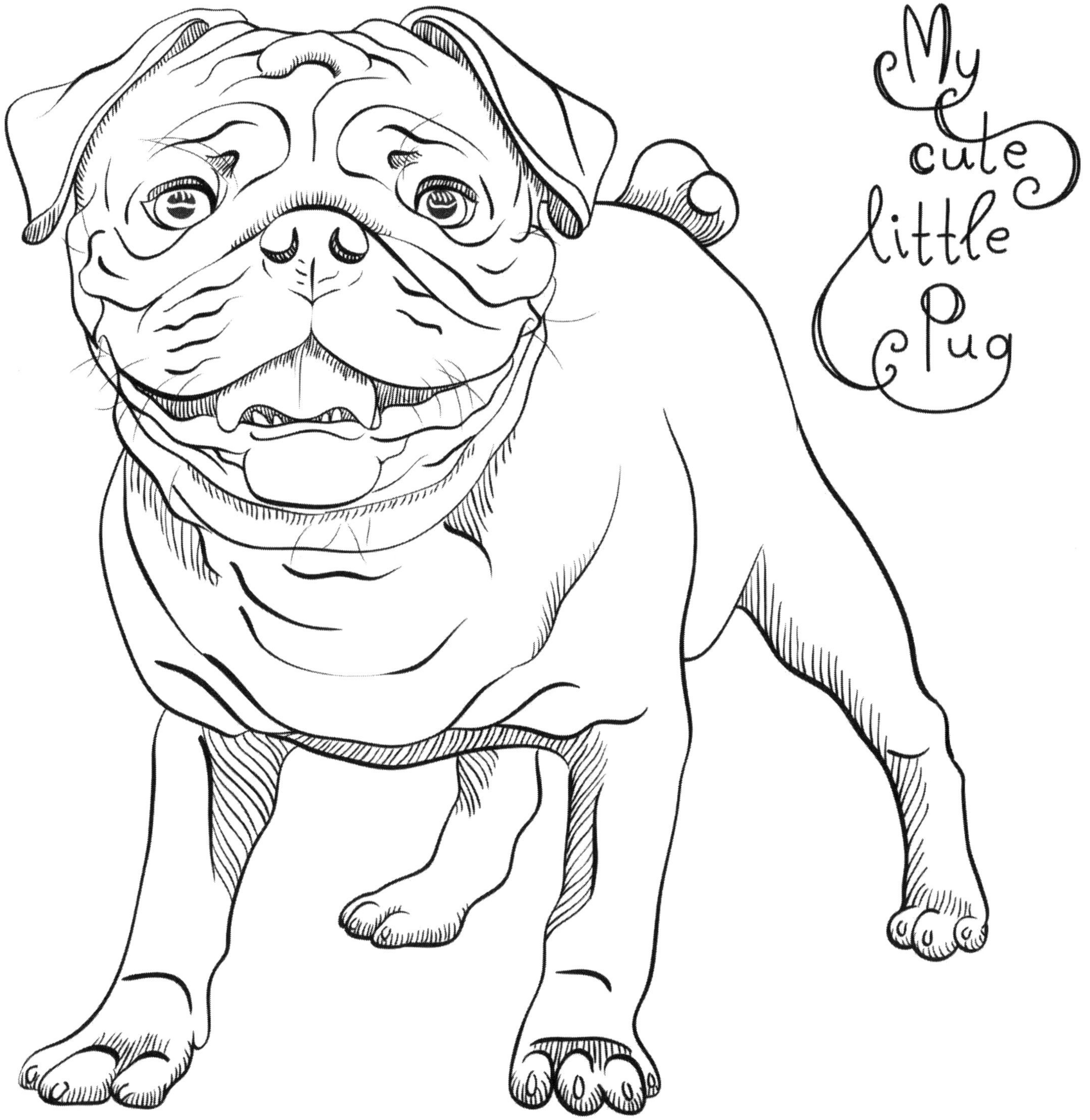
My cute little Pug

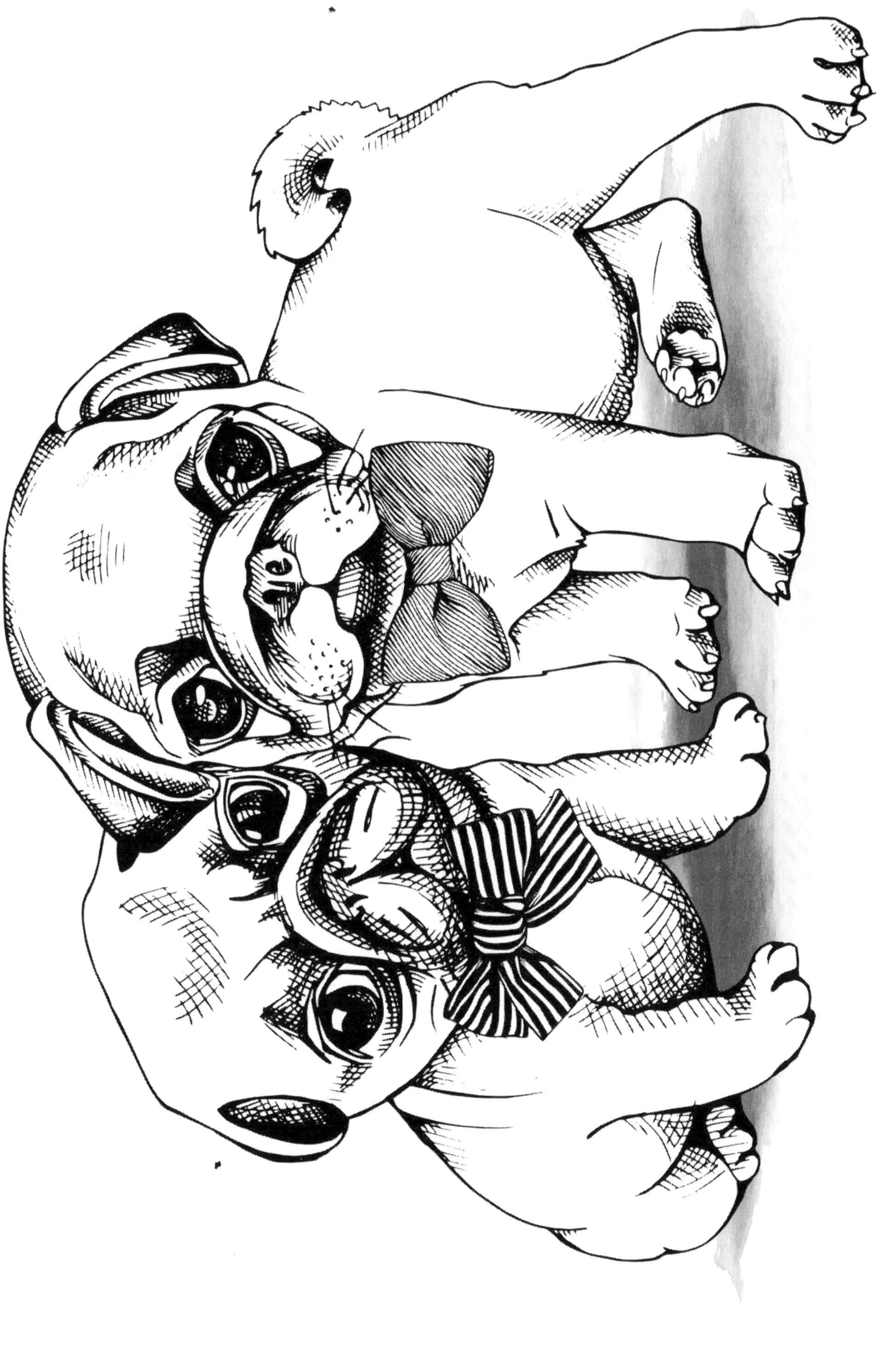

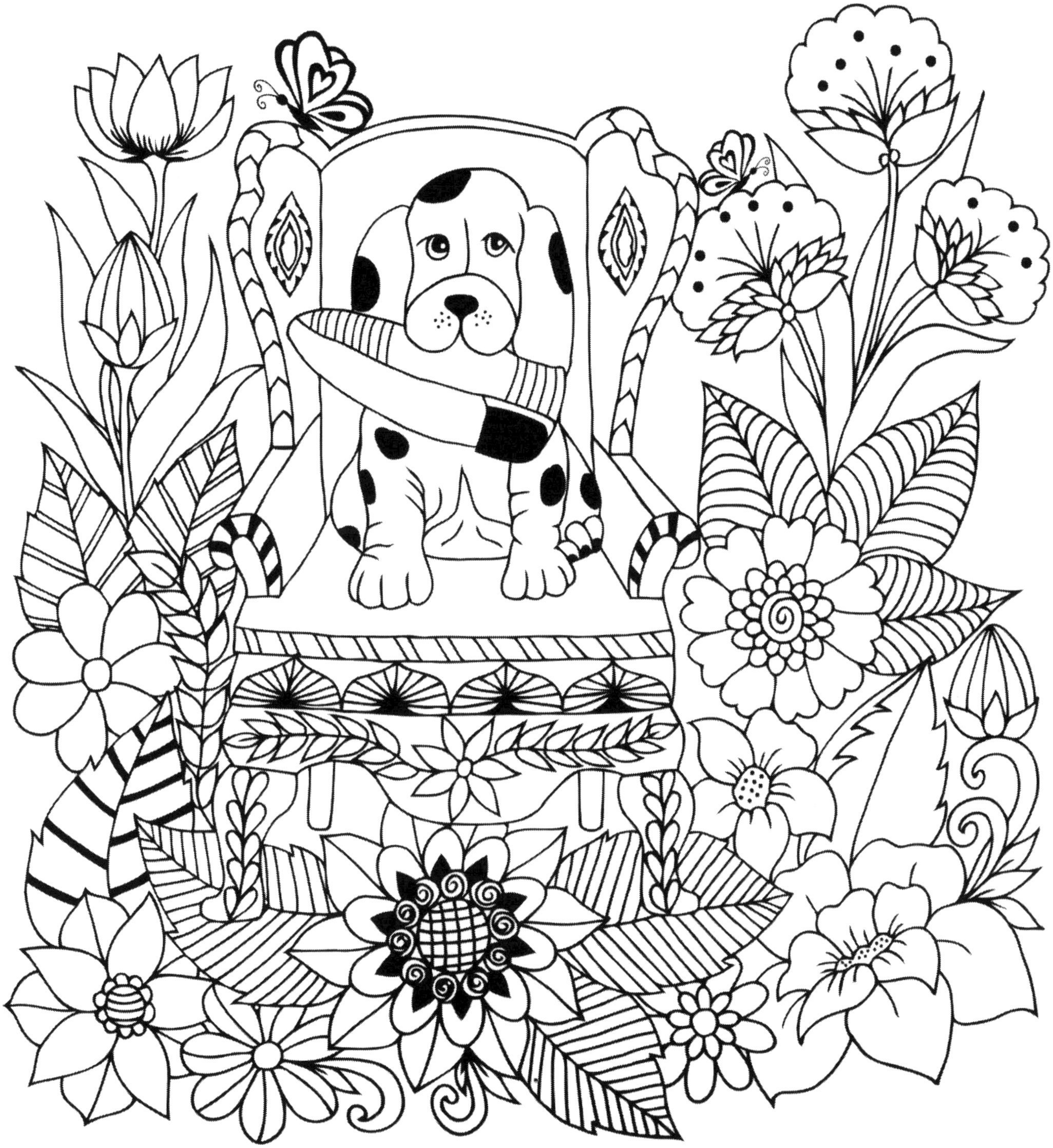

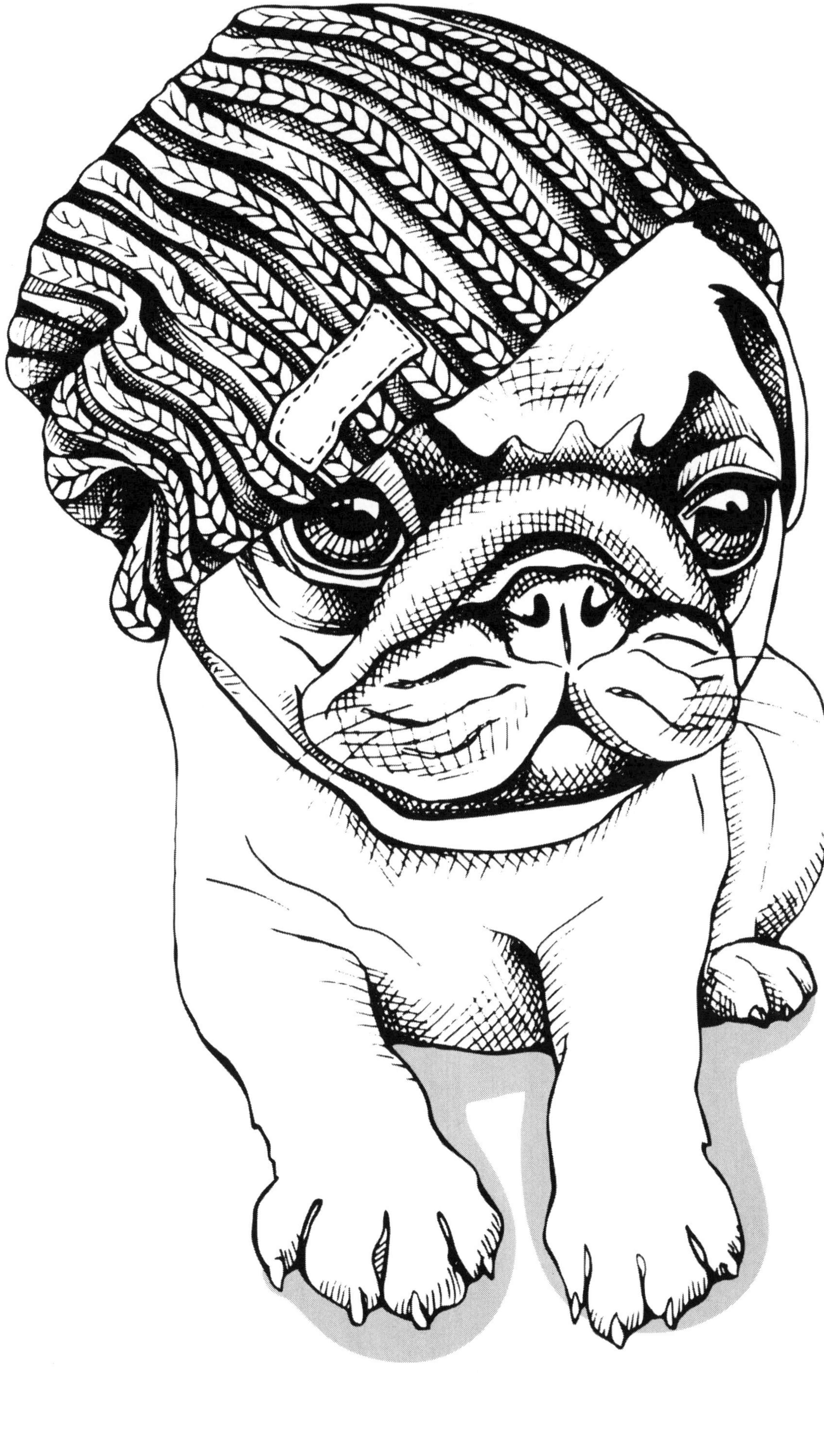

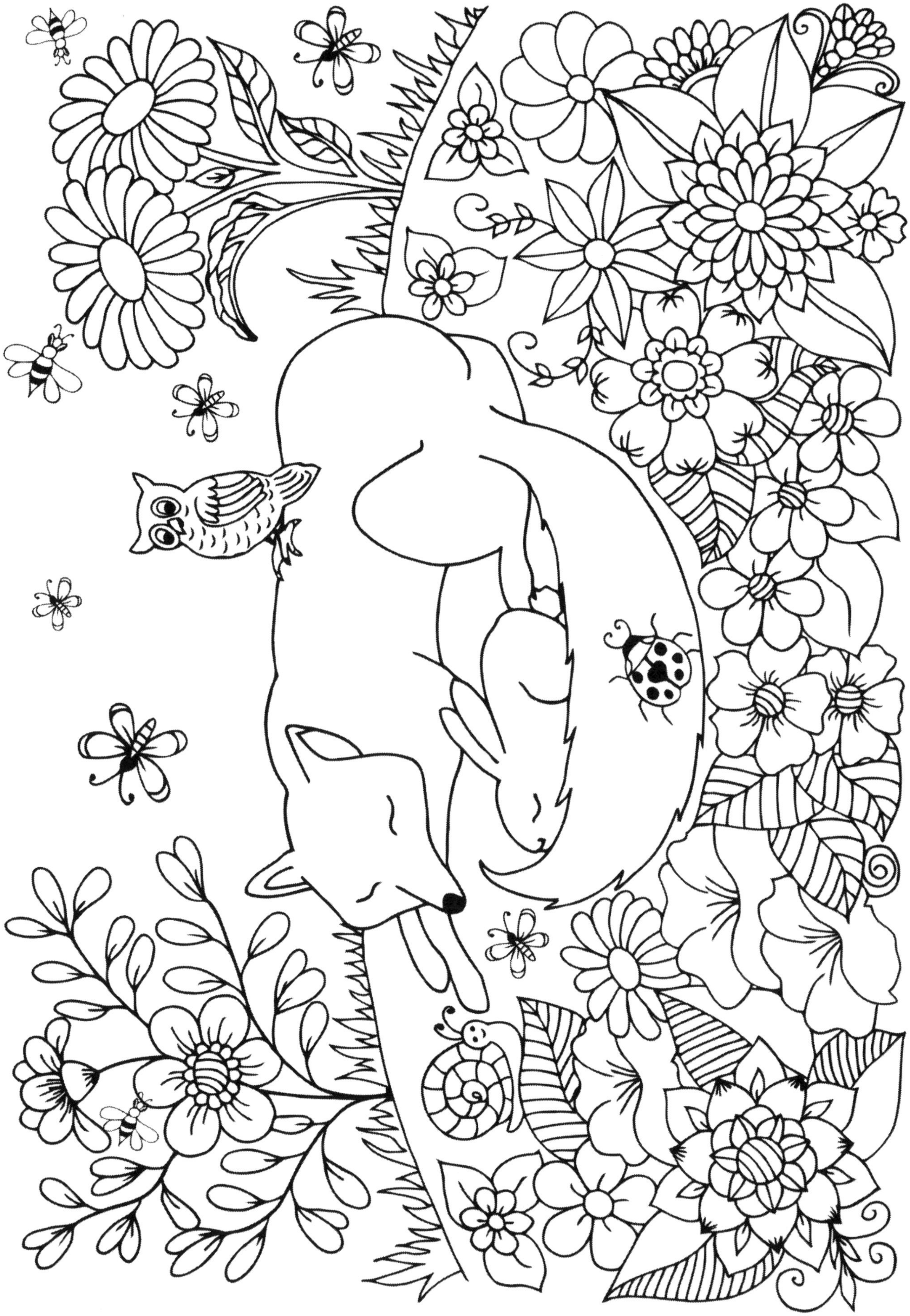

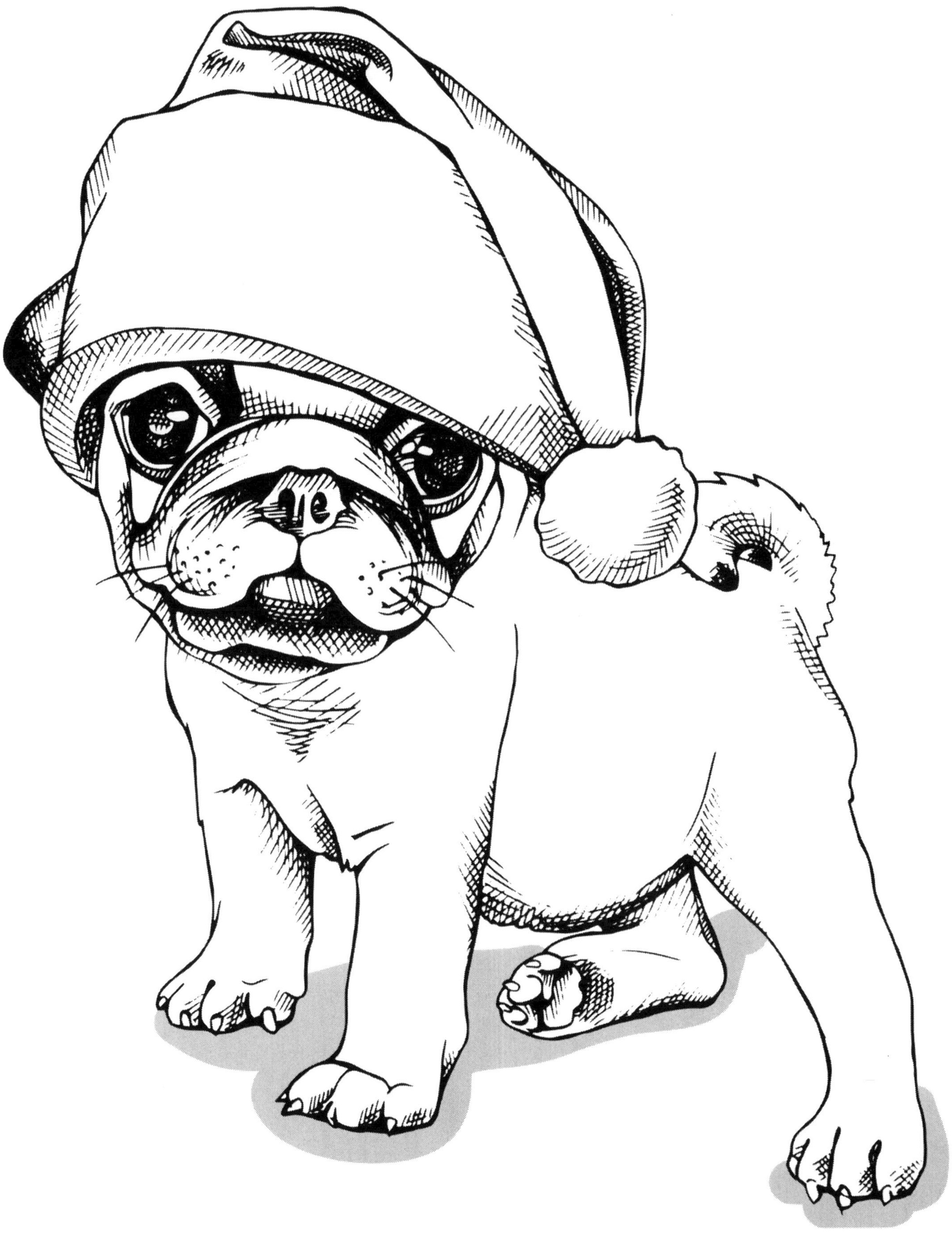

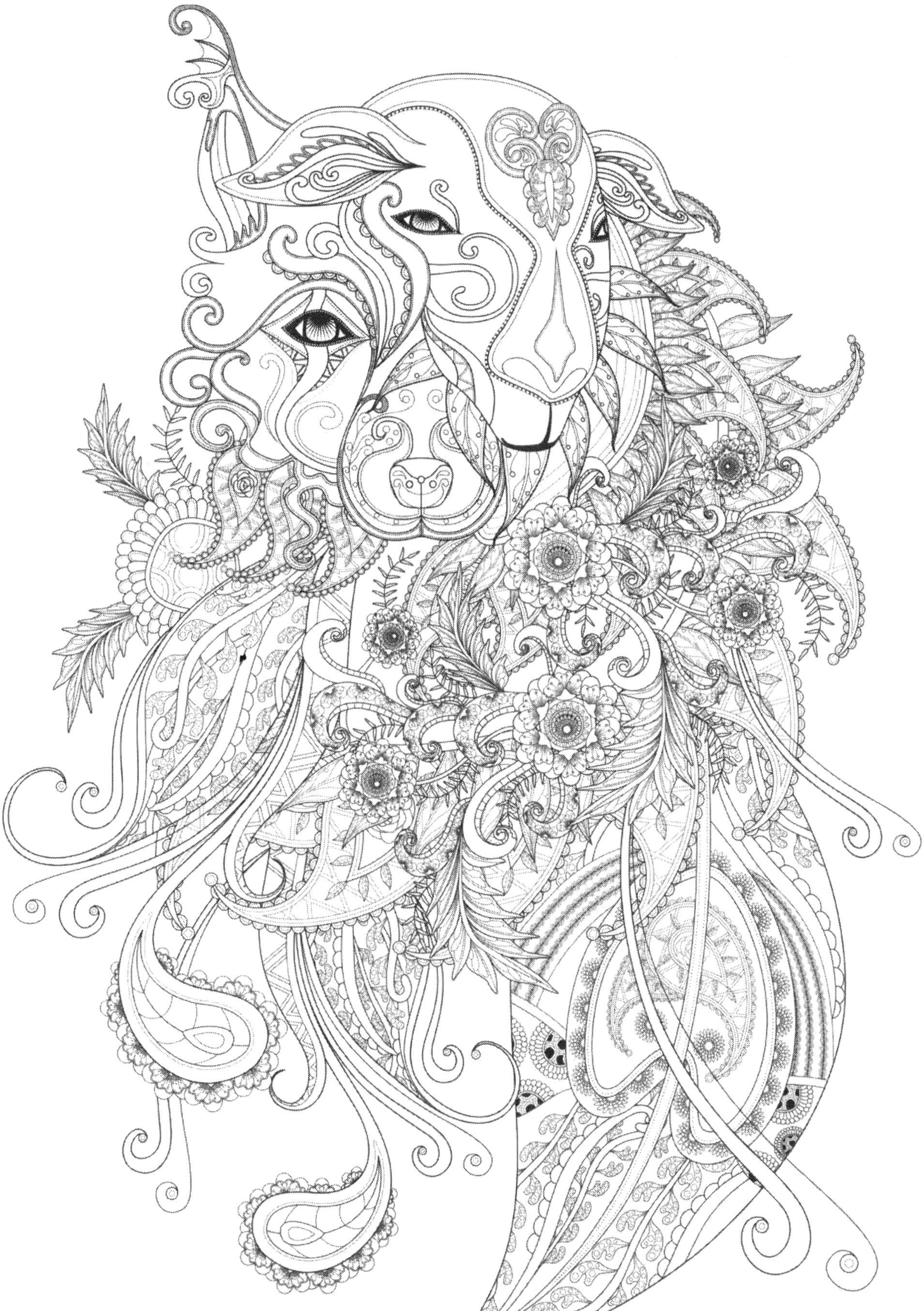

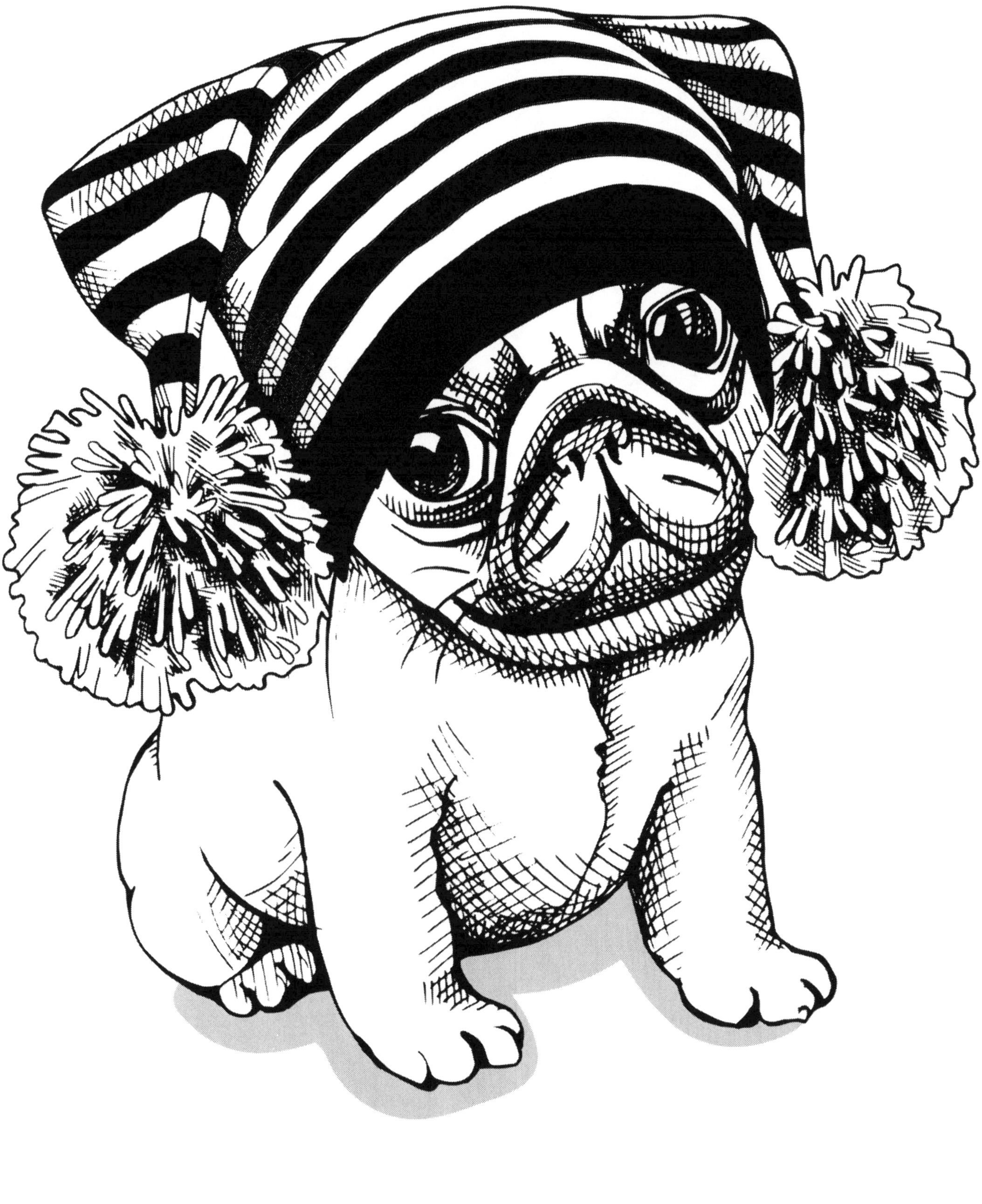

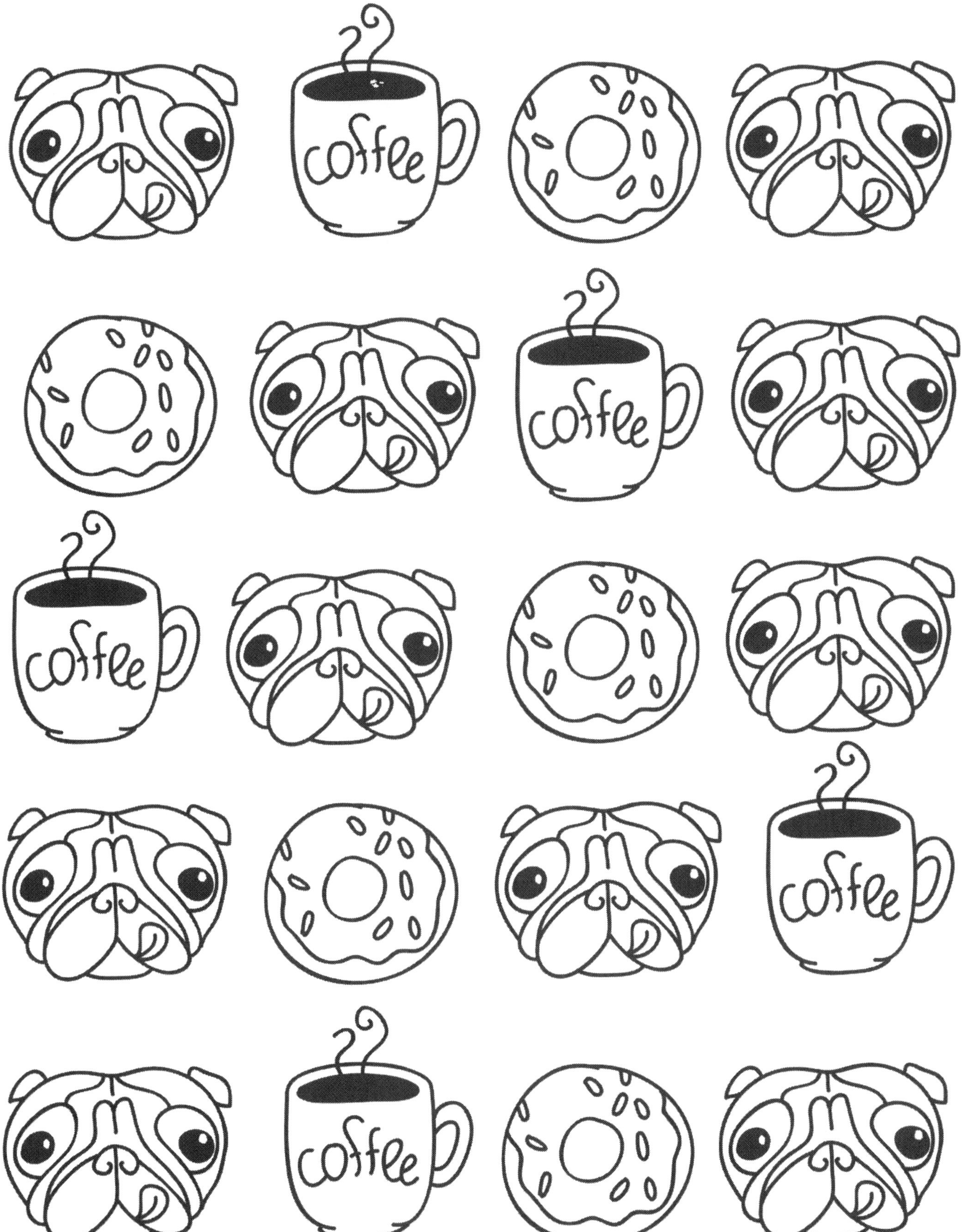
coffee
coffee
coffee
coffee
coffee

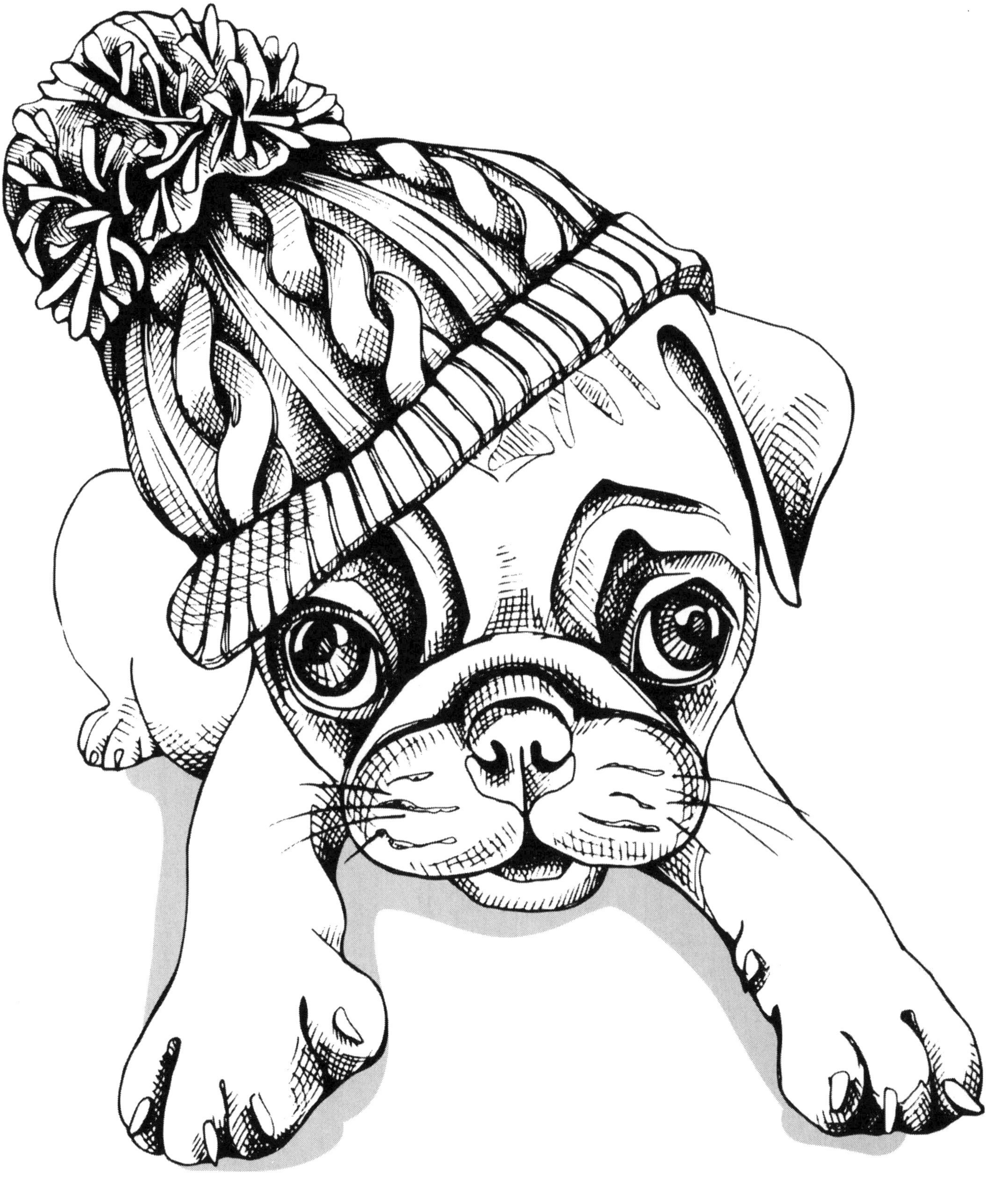

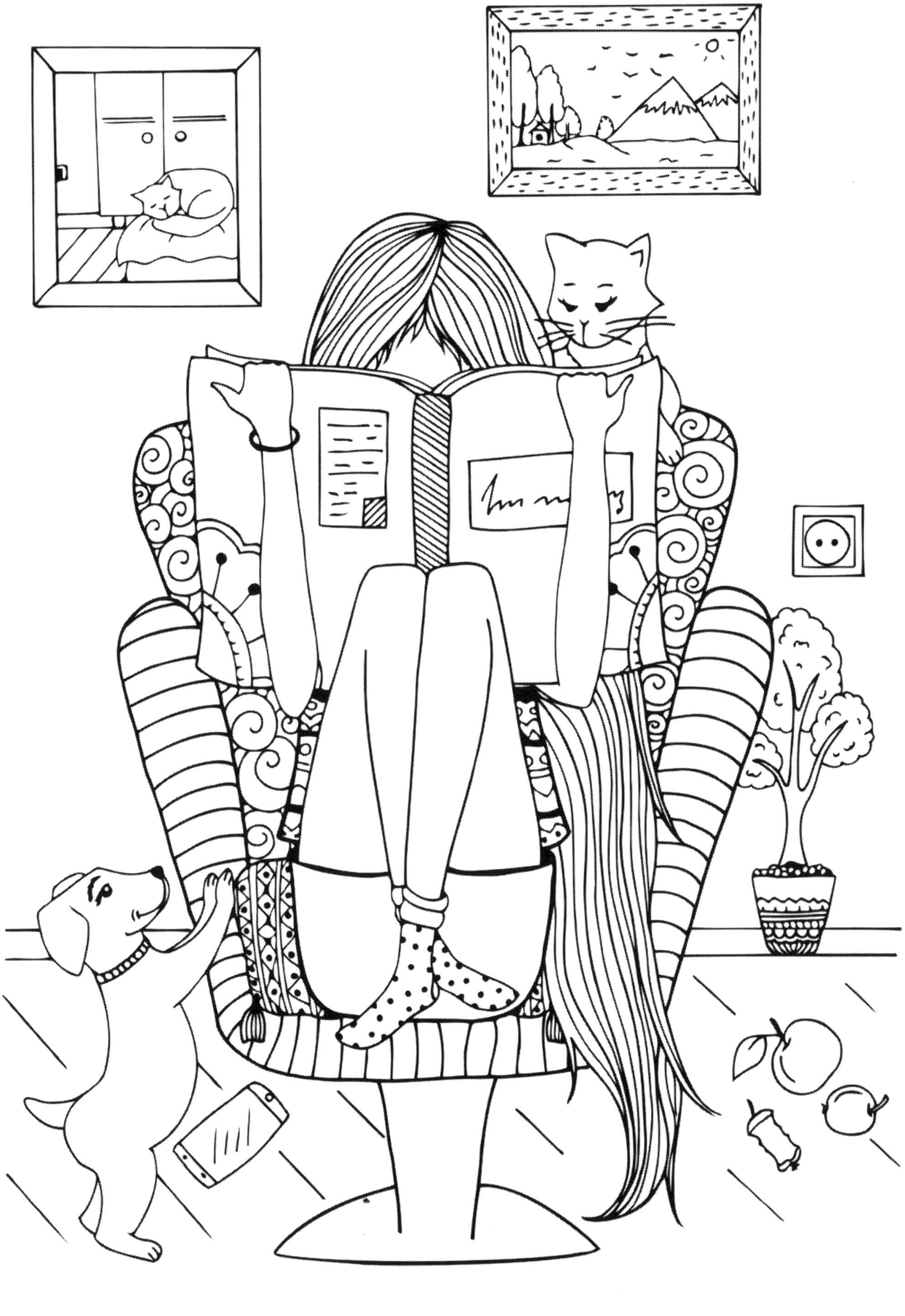

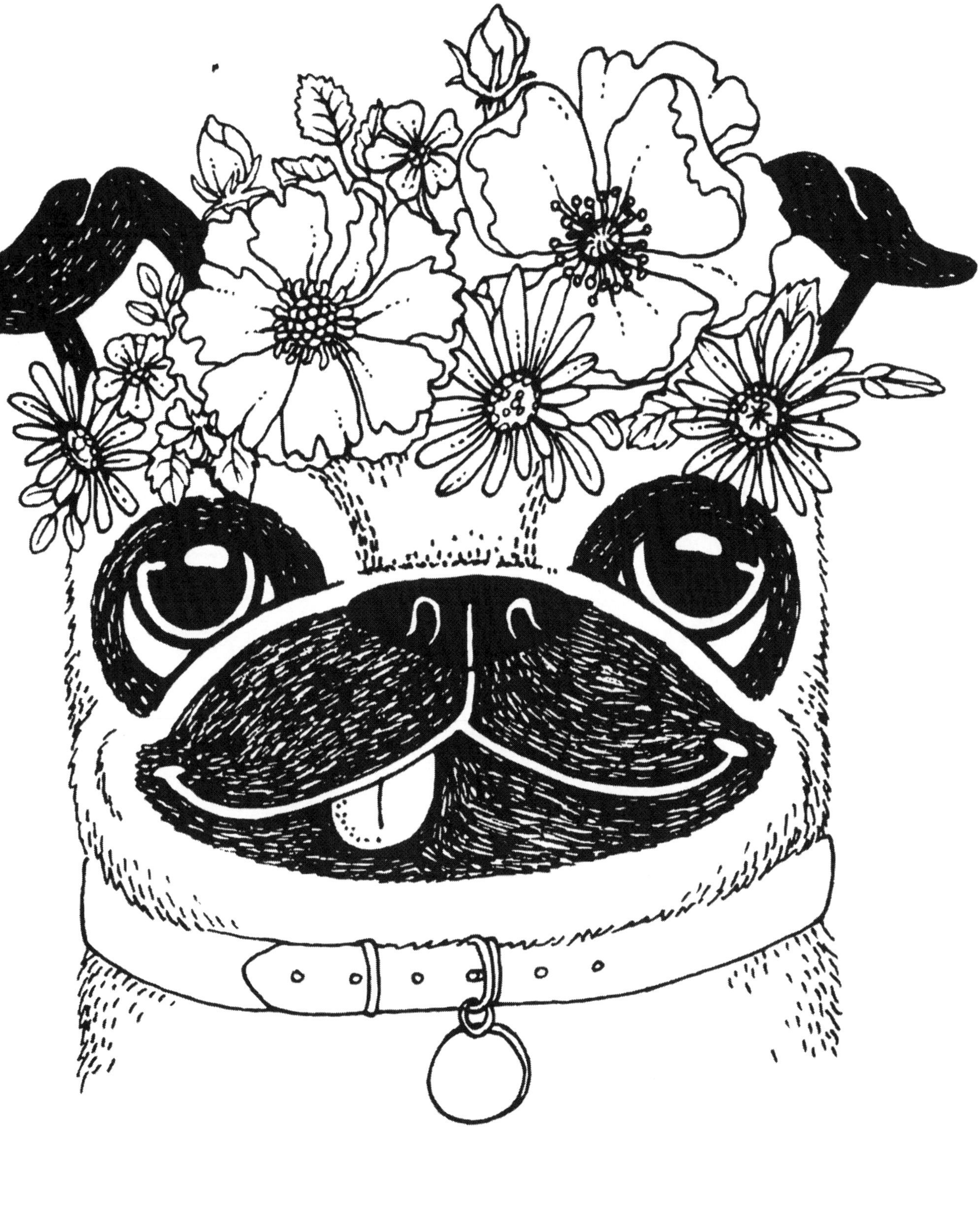

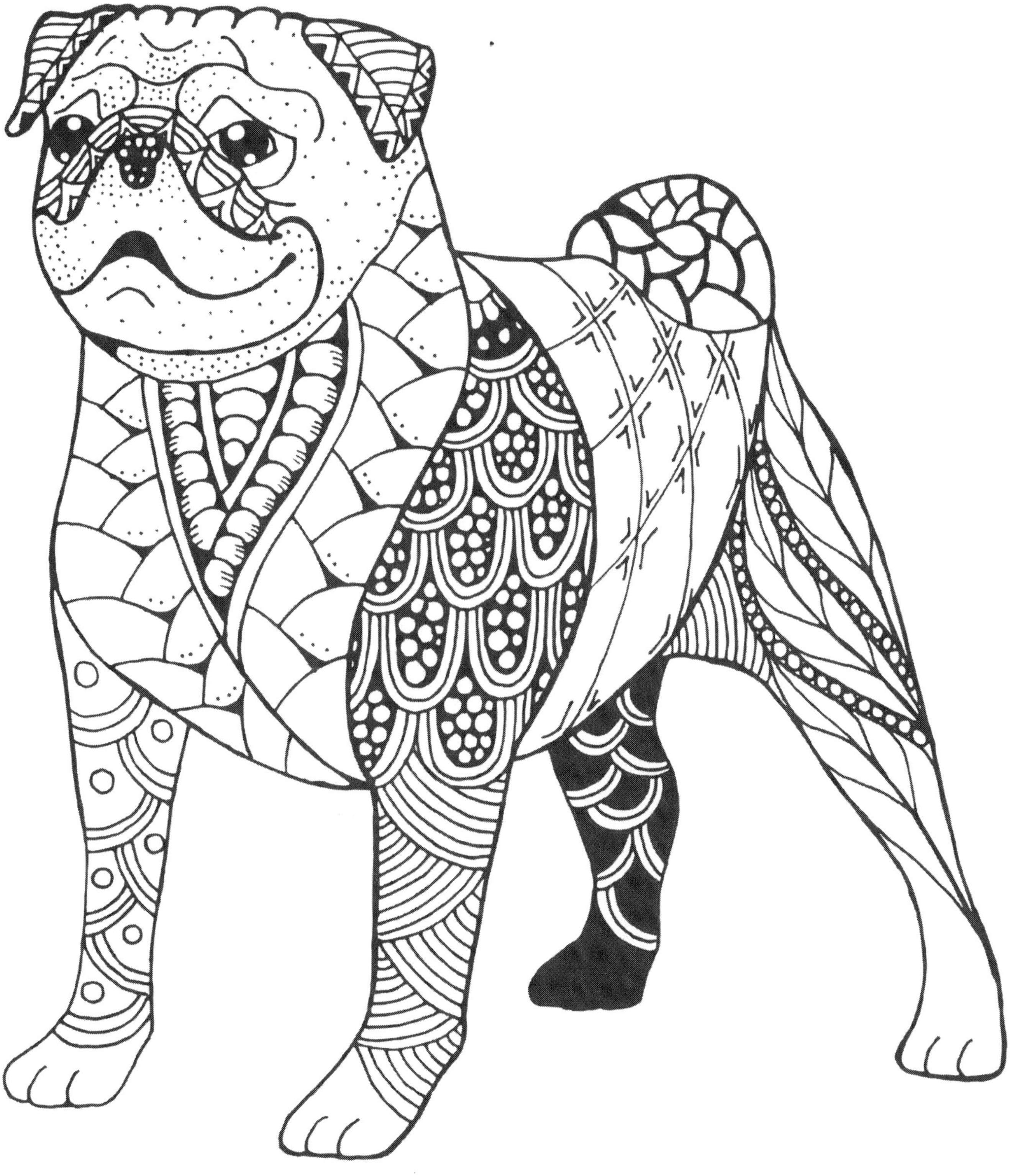

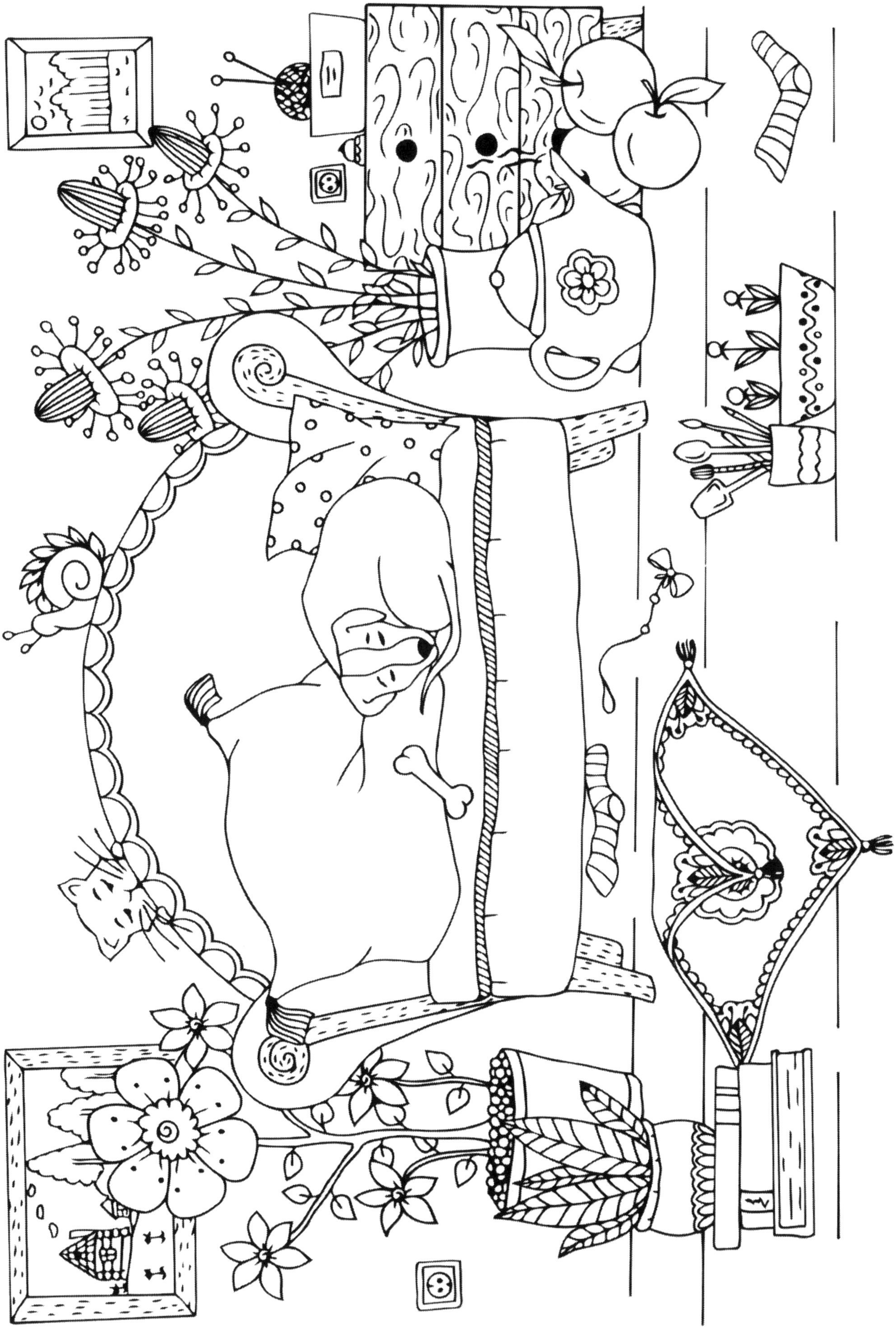

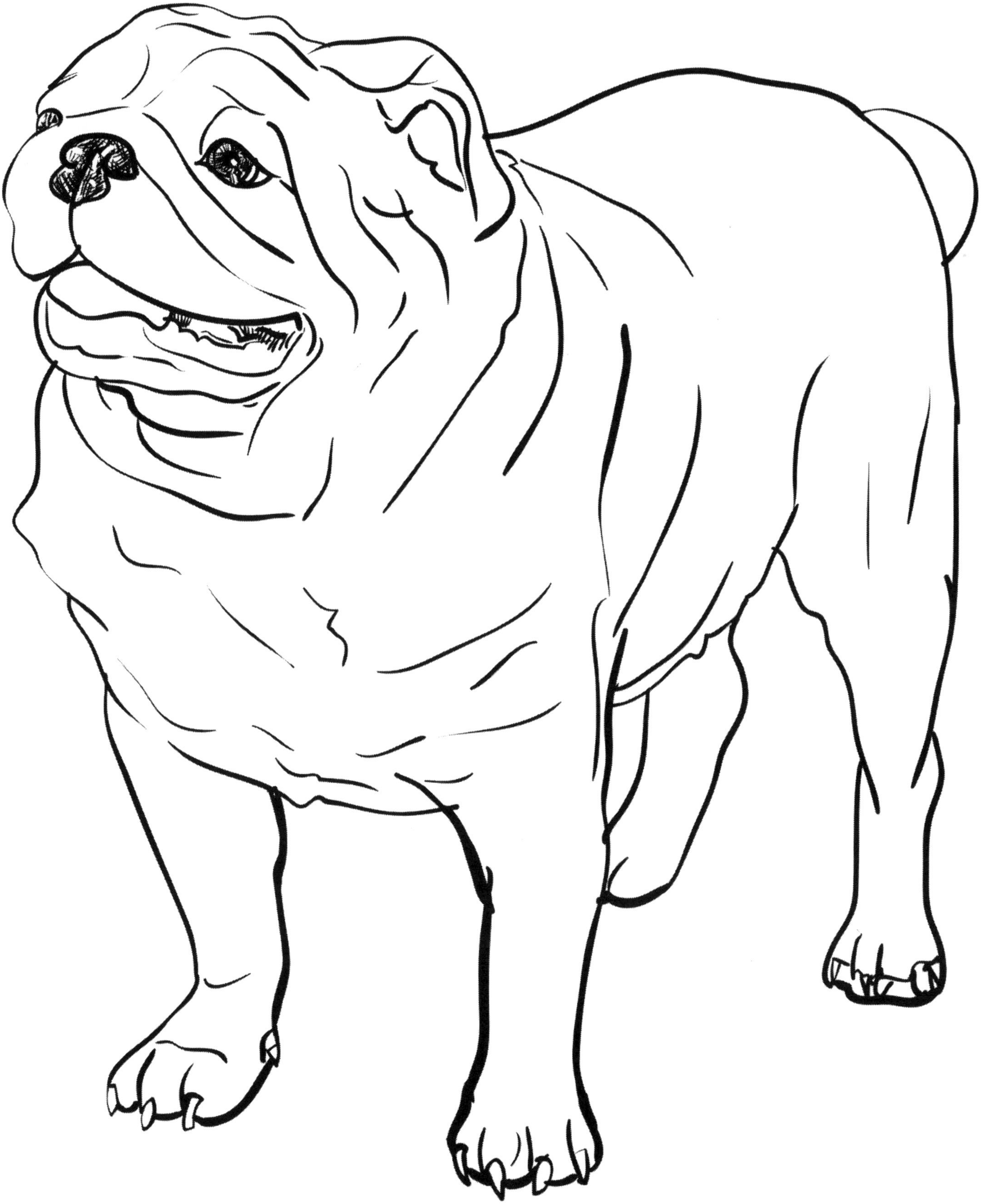

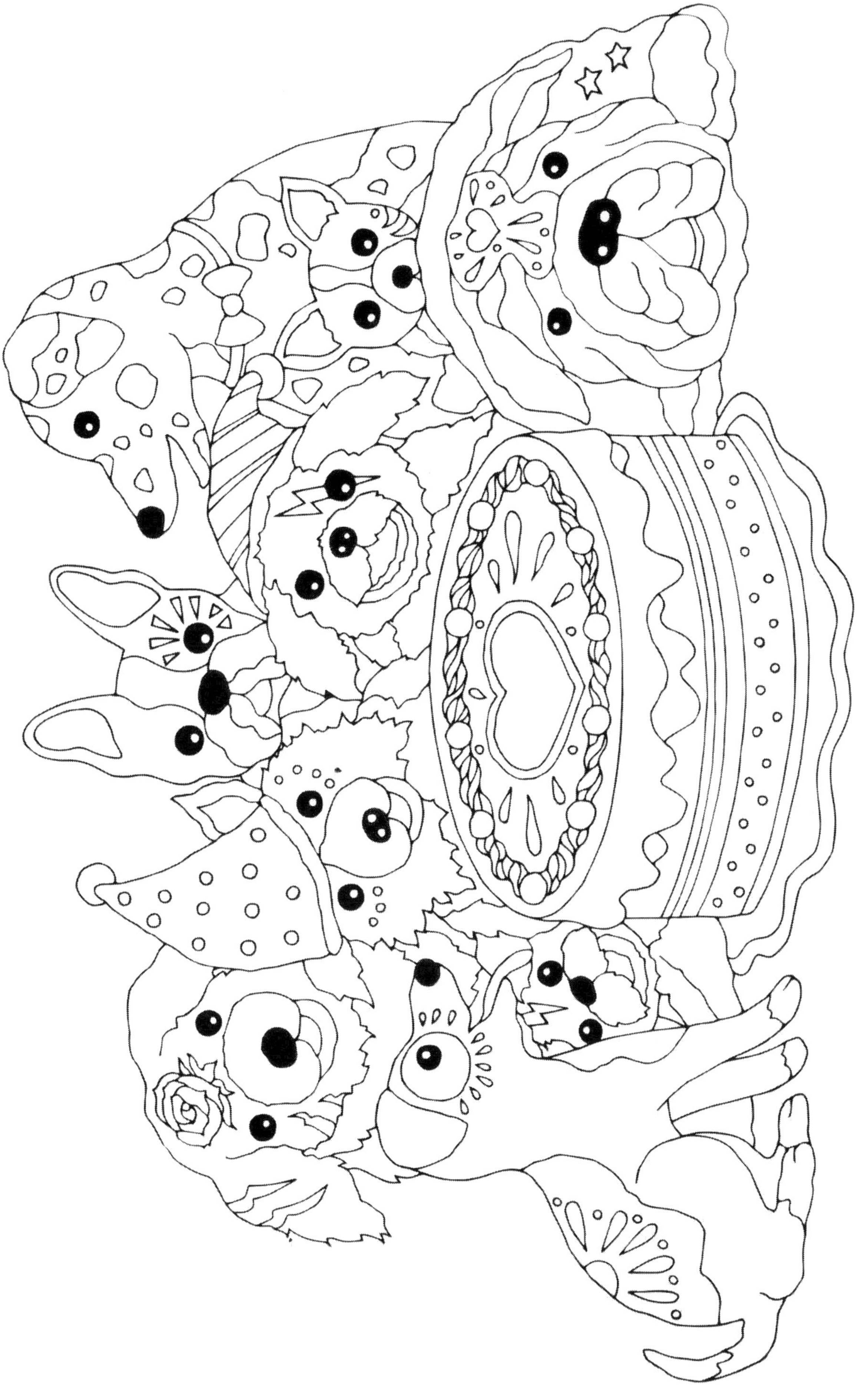

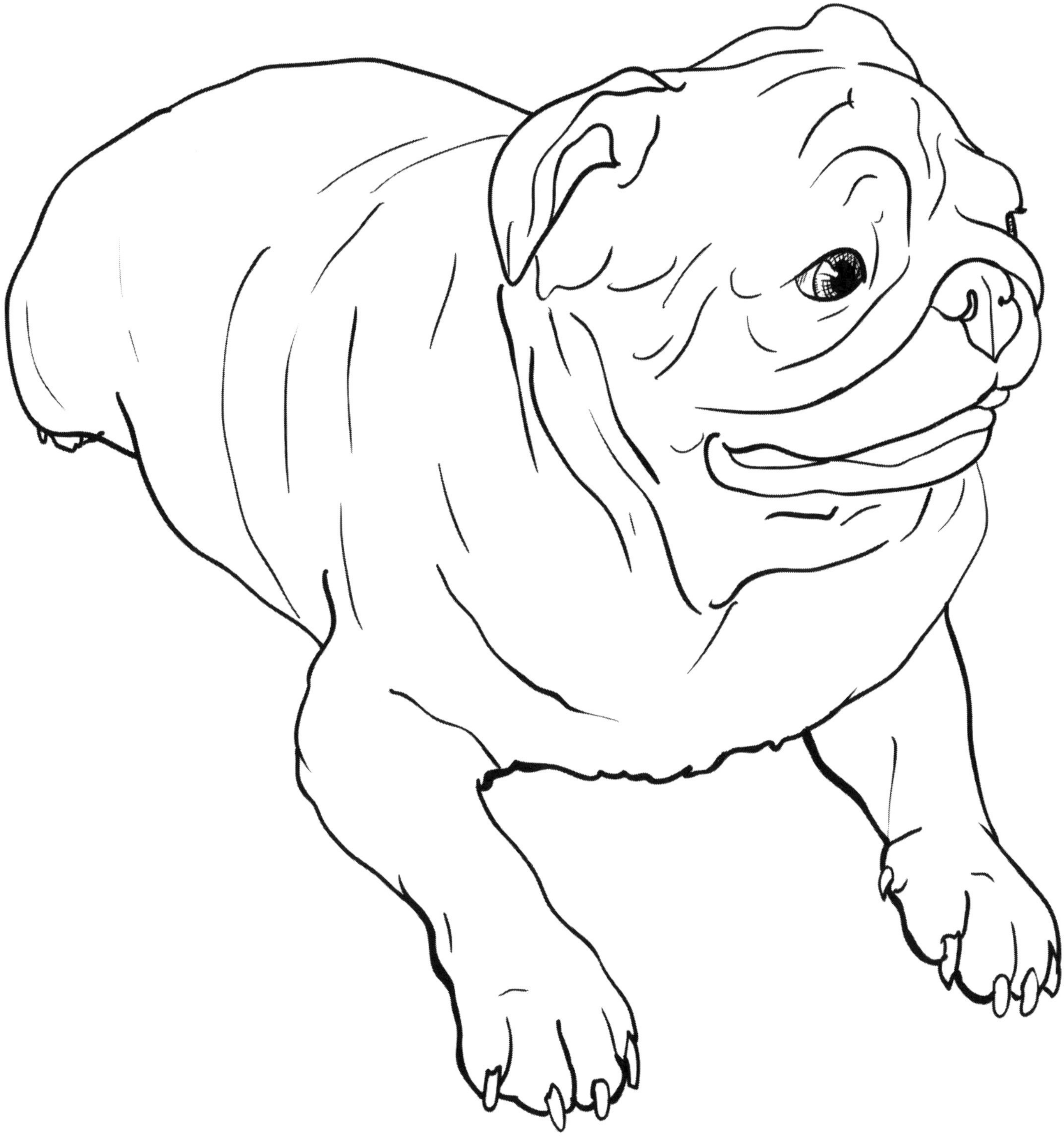

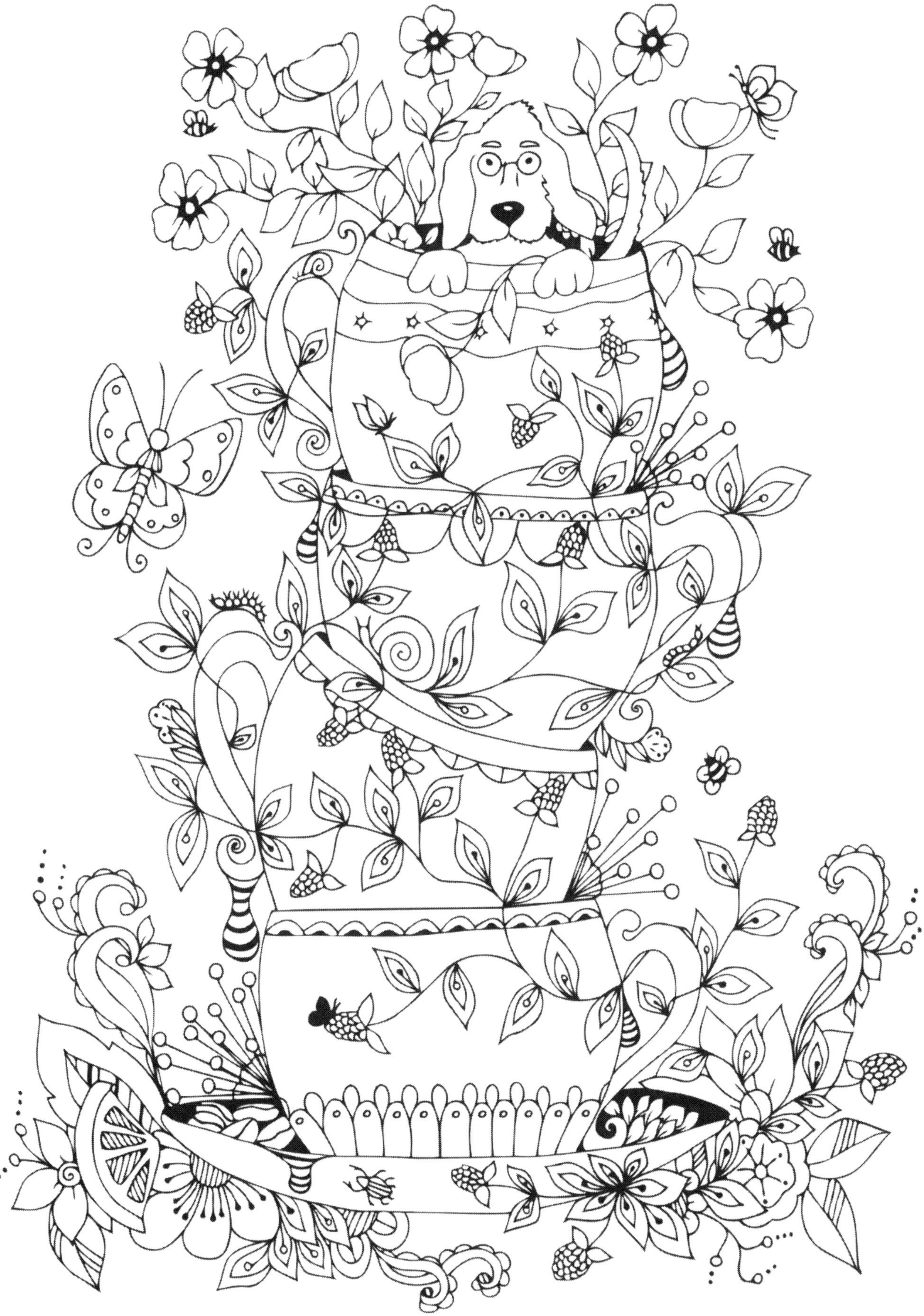

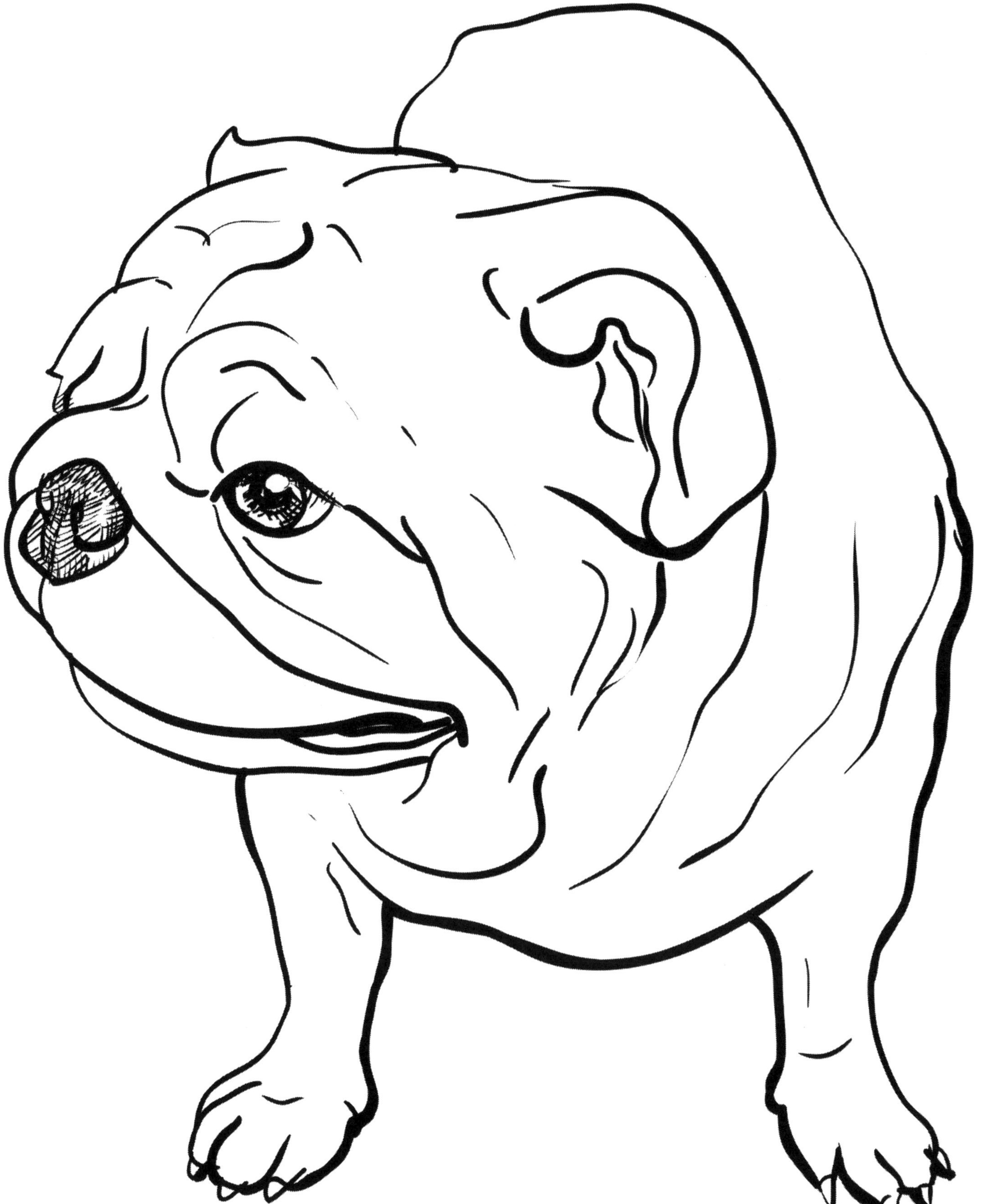

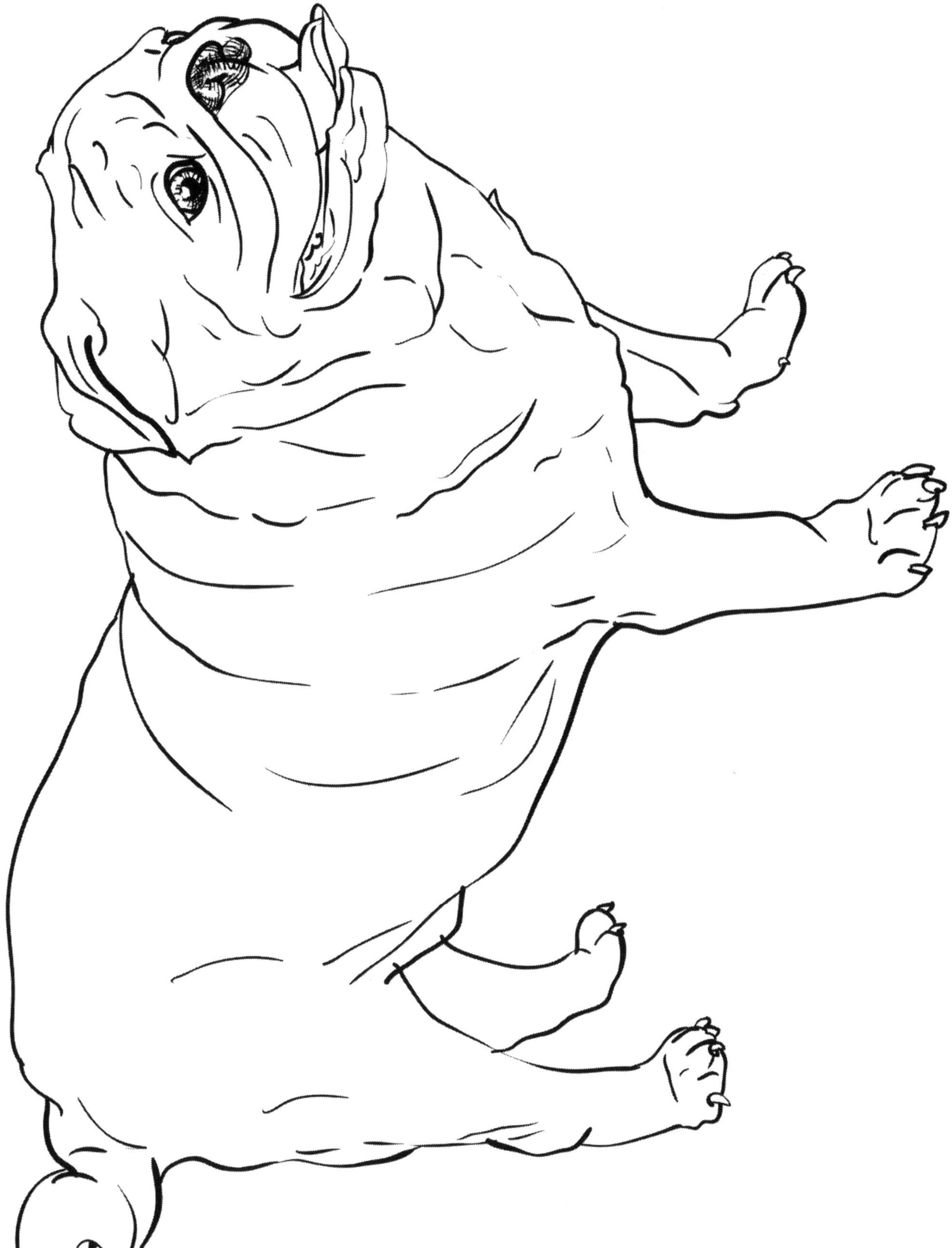

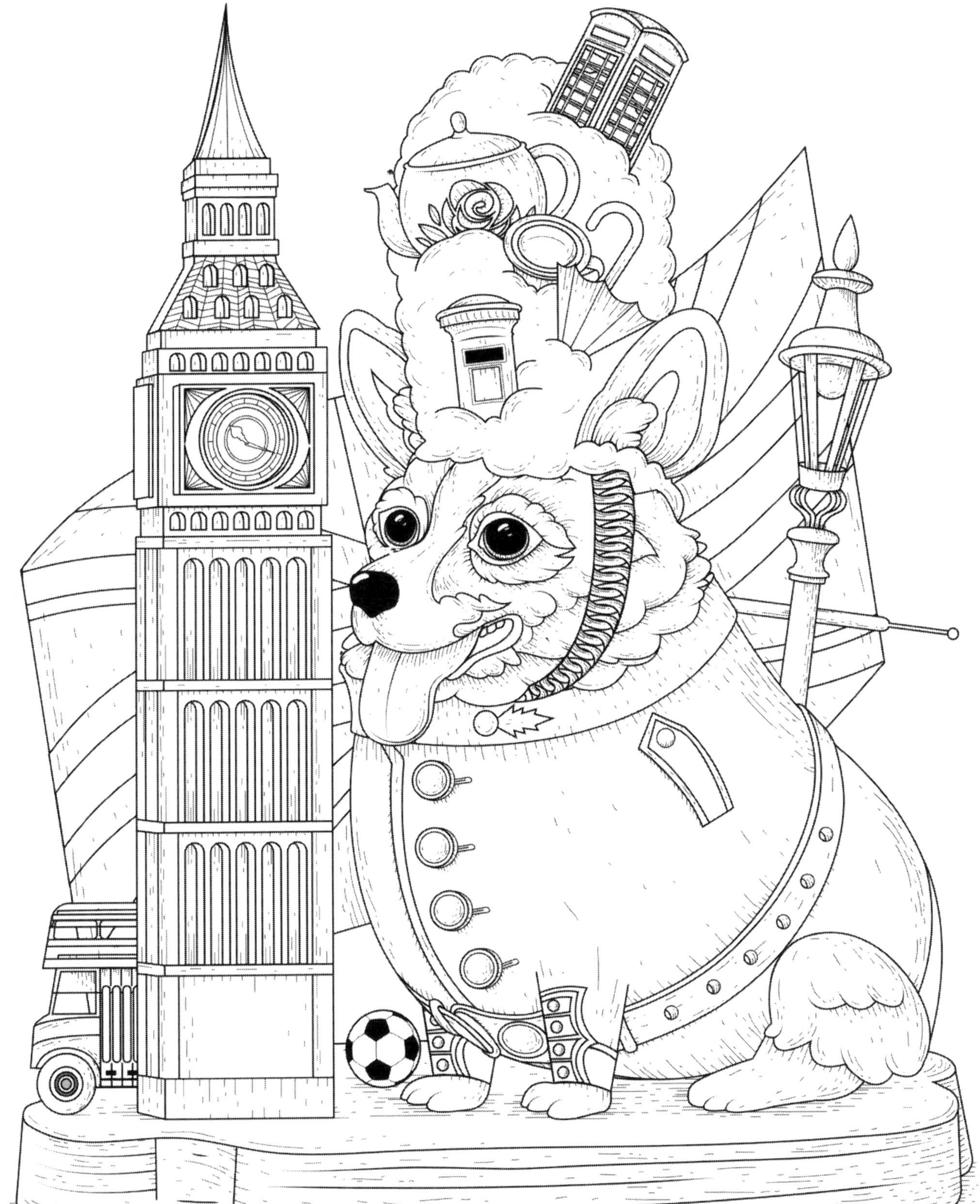

22157289R00043

Printed in Great Britain
by Amazon